CULTURES OF THE WORLD

Guyana

Leslie Jermyn and Winnie Wong

 Marshall Cavendish
Benchmark
New York

PICTURE CREDITS
Cover: © Getty Images
alt.type/Reuters: 34, 36, 41, 107, 119 • Audrius Tomonis: 135 • Boris Kester: 100 • Corbis: 11, 19, 88, 97, 124 •
Francis Tan: 131 • Getty Images: 56, 85, 104, 129 • Hutchison Library: 10, 92, 101, 102 • National Geographic
Society Images: 47, 52, 53 • North Wind Pictures Archives: 21 • Photolibrary: 1, 3, 5, 6, 7, 9, 12, 14, 15, 17, 18,
22, 23, 30, 31, 35, 38, 39, 40, 42, 43, 44, 46, 48, 49, 50, 51, 54, 58, 59, 60, 61, 63, 64, 65, 68, 70, 74, 75, 76, 78,
80, 81, 82, 83, 84, 89, 90, 91, 94, 96, 98, 99, 103, 105, 108, 109, 111, 114, 115, 116, 117, 118, 120, 125, 126 ,127,
128, 130 • Topfoto: 20, 25, 27, 28, 29 • Topham Picturepoint: 8 • Travel Ink: 49

PRECEDING PAGE
Children fishing at Lake Capoey in Guyana.

Publisher (U.S.): Michelle Bisson
Editors: Deborah Grahame, Mindy Pang
Copyreader: Tara Tomczyk
Designers: Nancy Sabato, Lock Hong Liang
Cover picture researcher: Connie Gardner
Picture researcher: Thomas Khoo

Marshall Cavendish Benchmark
99 White Plains Road
Tarrytown, NY 10591
Website: www.marshallcavendish.us

© Times Media Private Limited 2000
© Marshall Cavendish International (Asia) Private Limited 2011
® "Cultures of the World" is a registered trademark of Times Publishing Limited.

Originated and designed by Times Media Private Limited
An imprint of Marshall Cavendish International (Asia) Private Limited
A member of Times Publishing Limited

Marshall Cavendish is a trademark of Times Publishing Limited.

All Internet sites were correct and accurate at the time of printing. All monetary figures in this publication
are in U.S. dollars.

Library of Congress Cataloging-in-Publication Data
Jermyn, Leslie.
  Guyana / Leslie Jermyn and Winnie Wong. — 2nd ed.
    p. cm. — (Cultures of the world)
  Includes bibliographical references and index.
  Summary: "Provides comprehensive information on the geography, history,
    wildlife, governmental structure, economy, cultural diversity, peoples,
    religion, and culture of Guyana"--Provided by publisher.
  ISBN 978-1-60870-023-3
  1. Guyana—Juvenile literature. I. Wong, Winnie. II. Title.
  F2368.5.J47 2010
  988.1--dc22   2010000724

Printed in China
7 6 5 4 3 2 1

CONTENTS

INTRODUCTION

THE COOPERATIVE REPUBLIC OF GUYANA (PREVIOUSLY KNOWN as British Guiana) is a land of massive, pristine rain forests endowed with energetic rivers, breathtaking waterfalls, and diverse Amazonian wildlife. Against this backdrop of a rugged and unspoiled ecosystem, Guyana's history is filled with stories of struggles and pain. Wandering Caribbean Amerindians, European colonial masters, African slaves, and indentured laborers from East India, China, and Portugal have all left their marks in Guyana. Today their descendants number fewer than a million, and most live along the narrow coastal strip facing the Atlantic Ocean. Despite the political instability and interethnic tension, Guyana's diverse communities are focused on bringing the spectacular natural attributes of their country to their full potential, whether it is through ecotourism, sugar and rice exports, or the mining of bauxite, gold, and diamonds.

GEOGRAPHY

An aerial view of the rain forest and tributary to Kaieteur Falls in Guyana.

CHAPTER 1

THE COOPERATIVE REPUBLIC OF Guyana (gee-AH-nah), or Guyana for short, is one of three small countries located in the northeast of the South American continent. The country has an area of 83,000 square miles (214,969 square kilometers), about the same size as Great Britain or slightly smaller than Idaho.

Guyana is bounded on the north by the tropical Atlantic Ocean, on the southeast by Suriname, on the south and southwest by Brazil, and on the northwest by Venezuela.

Apart from infertile soil, the main reason people do not want to live in the highlands is the lack of transportation and services.

The spectacular 822-foot-high (250-meter-high) Kaieteur Falls on the Potaro River.

The capital city, Georgetown, is located on the Atlantic coast. Guyana is a tropical country with rainy and dry seasons, and other minor seasonal temperature change. Several important rivers flow across a land that is rich in plant and animal life.

GEOGRAPHIC REGIONS

Guyana is part of a large region known as the Guianas (gee-AH-nahs) that includes Suriname and French Guiana. In the late 17th and 18th century, eastern Venezuela and northern Brazil were part of the Guianas as well. The region is characterized by great river systems and

Bartica on the Essequibo River seen from the air.

high annual rainfall. Four main natural and climatic zones can be distinguished within Guyana's boundaries—the coast, the forests, the savannah, and the mountains.

THE COASTAL ZONE This is the narrow strip of land bordering the Atlantic Ocean where most of Guyana's economic activities take place. The coastal zone stretches 285 miles (459 km) from Venezuela to Suriname and varies in width from 10 miles (16 km) up to 40 miles (64 km) along major rivers. Although this zone represents only 4 percent of total land area, it is very fertile. Thus it is where most Guyanese people live and where the two main crops, sugarcane and rice, are intensely cultivated.

Guyana is bordered by the ocean on one side and swamps inland, making it very susceptible to floods. Some of this area would normally lie 4 to 5 feet (1.2 to 1.5 m) below sea level, but it is protected by a complicated system of around 140 miles of dikes and seawalls. The coastal zone also has high annual rainfall of 70 to 110 inches (178 to 279 centimeters), which further increases the chances of flooding.

STAYING DRY ON THE COAST

The densely settled and farmed coastal strip is sandwiched between the Atlantic Ocean on one side and swamps on the other. Much of this land lies below sea level. In order to keep the land dry, the Guyanese have built and maintained a complicated system of walls, sluices, and canals to control flooding.

The first part of the system is a large seawall that prevents the sea from flooding this part of the shore. The wall is equipped with sluice gates that regulate the outflow of water back to the sea and from inland swamps to the sea. At the rear of the coastal strip is another wall or dam that prevents swamp water from flooding the settled zone. Between these two dams is a complex network of canals and trenches that move water through the area for irrigation and drainage.

The canals and trenches are of two different levels. The high canals are used for irrigation and transportation, while the low trenches are for drainage. These canals and trenches must be kept clean of silt (fine sand that can clog water systems) and plants. Maintaining the system is the responsibility of both the government and the people. The Public Works Department undertakes major repairs to the canals and trenches, but local communities are responsible for maintaining the sluices and cleaning plant life out of the canals. Without hard work and cooperation, life on the coast would be impossible.

MAGNIFICENT WATERFALLS

Guyana boasts of some of the highest and most beautiful waterfalls in the world. Kaieteur Falls, on the Potaro River, is a spectacular 822 feet (251 m) high. It consists of two falls, a small one of 81 feet (25 m) and a larger one of 820 feet (250 m). By comparison, Niagara Falls—located between the borders of Ontario, Canada, and New York, United States—is only 193 feet (59 m) high. Kaieteur Falls is a major tourist attraction because of its sheer size and the beautiful prismatic colors that form with the mist rising off the water. It is also home to martins and swallows that nest behind the curtain of water; they can be seen swooping home after foraging for food in the surrounding forests.

The name Kaieteur comes from an indigenous language and means "Old Man's Fall." Legend has it that an old chieftain offered himself to the Great Spirit for the good of his people. He paddled his canoe over the edge of the falls and was turned to stone. It is said that you can see his stone canoe when there is a drought and the water level is low. Despite the magnificent size of Kaieteur, it is not the biggest waterfall in Guyana. Two other falls are higher—King George VI Falls on the Utshi River, at 1,600 feet (488 m), and King Edward Falls on the Semang River, at 840 feet (256 m). However, these are not popular tourist attractions because they are hard to reach. Many of Guyana's rivers have smaller falls and rapids that are more accessible from the coast, such as Orinduik Falls on the Ireng River at the Brazilian border.

THE FOREST ZONE Covering over 66,000 square miles (170,940 square km), the forest zone makes up the largest portion of the country and stretches from the coastal zone to the interior. As the name implies, it is heavily forested. Few people live here because the soil, which is made up of brown and white sands and clays, is not suitable for growing food crops. The land in this zone rises gently from sea level, and the area is crisscrossed with large rivers that empty into the Atlantic Ocean.

The four largest rivers found in Guyana will include the Demerara, Essequibo, Courantyne, and Berbice. As these rivers flow from their sources high in the mountains to the ocean, the shift in altitude results in dramatic rapids, cataracts, and waterfalls. Guyana has some of the continent's most spectacular waterfalls, and these are popular tourist destinations.

The world's largest water lily, the Regis water lily, is found on the Rupununi River in Guyana.

THE SAVANNAH ZONE The savannah zone is an area of high grasslands located in the far southwest of the country near the border with Brazil. The largest savannah area is called Rupununi, after the river of the same name that runs through the region. Totaling about 5,792 square miles (15,001 square km), the Rupununi Savannah is divided in half by the Kanuku Mountains.

The area is sparsely settled, although some Guyanese have cattle ranches there, and a few indigenous groups make their homes on the savannah. There is a second, smaller savannah approximately 100 miles (161 km) southeast of Georgetown. Located in the Upper Berbice River, the Intermediate Savannah consists of 615,000 acres (248,882 hectares) of grass terrain with forestlands dissected by numerous rivers and streams.

MYSTERIOUS RORAIMA

Mount Roraima is actually a mesa or plateau, rather than a mountain. It is part of a vast 200,000-square-mile (518,000-square-km) region of sandstone mesas that cover the western bulge of Guyana (above the "waist" where the country narrows) and parts of Venezuela and Brazil. These plateaus are said to be the remains of a large sandstone deposit that covered this region 1.8 billion years ago. The rock is so old that it predates the time when South America and Africa parted to form separate continents 135 million years ago.

Over the millennia water erosion from many rivers has carved deep ravines and valleys into the mesas. Roraima is the highest of the plateaus. Its name in a native language means "singing of waterfalls," which is an apt description, because there are many streams of water plunging off its edges to the lowlands below. This region is mostly unexplored because of the difficult terrain.

The first expedition to reach the top of Roraima was led by Everard Im Thurn, a British botanist, in 1884. Im Thurn brought back samples of plant life that had never been recorded before. The plateaus are isolated because of their height, and this has allowed plants and animals to evolve and thrive in an ecological niche that is not found anywhere else in the world.

There is even one species of toad that is related to a species in Africa, which suggests that there was once a common ancestor for both when the continents were joined about 120 million years ago. This toad, Oreophrynella quelchii, *has not needed to evolve much in this isolated environment, and it can neither hop nor swim. When Im Thurn lectured about this isolated region after his return to England, Arthur Conan Doyle (the creator of Sherlock Holmes) was inspired to write a novel about an expedition in which prehistoric plants and dinosaurs are discovered living high up on Roraima. The book, called* The Lost World, *was published in 1912.*

Today, even with modern technology such as helicopters, much of Roraima's 44 square miles (114 square km) remains unexplored.

THE MOUNTAINOUS ZONE Along the borders with Venezuela and Brazil are the Pakaraima Mountains. This area is characterized by sharply stepped plateaus rising from the savannah plains below. It is the least-settled and least-known region of Guyana. There are believed to be some gold and diamond deposits in the mountains, but due to the lack of transportation, only few people from the coast have made the journey to try their luck.

The highest point in this range, and in Guyana, is Mount Roraima at 9,301 feet (2,835 m) high. It is located at the point where Venezuela, Brazil, and Guyana meet. Other mountain ranges in Guyana include the Kanuku Mountains (3,000 feet/914 m), and the Merume Mountains whose highest peak, Mount Caburai, is 4,806 feet (1,465 m).

CLIMATE

Because Guyana is situated close to the equator, temperatures are high throughout the year. The average daily temperature is 80°F (27°C), with a range of 74°F to 86°F (23°C to 30°C) between night and day. For most people living on the coast, these temperatures are moderated by the constant northeast trade winds that blow off the Atlantic Ocean.

The rain forest landscape and mangrove banks of the Kamuni River in Guyana.

Four seasons, defined by the amount of rainfall, can be distinguished in Guyana. Between mid-April and late July there is heavy rainfall. This is followed by a dry season that lasts until November, when another period of lighter rainfall begins. This third season lasts until February, when there is another dry season.

The average annual rainfall in Guyana is 90 inches (229 cm), with a range from a low of 60 inches (152 cm) to a high of 120 inches (305 cm), depending on the area and the year. Even during the dry season, however, the humidity in the air is very high, averaging about 70 percent. Seasonal drought can occur in July and August when the southeast trade wind bypasses the interior. This watery climate has influenced many aspects of life in Guyana, including crop production, dress, design of houses, and the annual cycle of social events.

PLANTS AND ANIMALS

Guyana boasts of extraordinary diversity in plant and animal life. From the sea to the deep Amazon regions, there are different ecosystems that support as many as 1,500 species of plants, insects, reptiles, amphibians, fish, 500 birds, and 200 mammals.

There are three main types of forests in Guyana—mangrove, hardwood, and tropical. Mangrove forests grow along the boundary between fresh water and salt water and survive in a mixture of the two known as brine. Mangroves can be found behind the settled coastal band in the swampy areas where rivers drain into the sea. From there, inland to the first line of cataracts on the major rivers, lies hardwood forest. Forest trees have adapted to living in sandy soil by extending their roots outward to capture water. Tropical forests extend from the cataracts to the border with Brazil

UNDERWATER WORLD

One of the inhabitants of Guyana's rivers is a kind of fish measuring 7 feet (2 m) in length and weighing 200 pounds (91 kilograms). This is the famous arapaima *(ah-rah-PAI-mah), a freshwater fish related to the salmon. The arapaima inhabits rivers in the highlands and savannahs and is sought by indigenous people and sportsmen alike. Arapaima are hunted with harpoons rather than lines and hooks because the fish is so big and strong, it can drag a fisherman off the bank of a river. Another freshwater giant is the endangered carnivorous black caiman. This reptile, the world's largest alligator species, can reach up to at least 13 feet (4 m) in length.*

The anaconda is a type of boa constrictor that prefers to live partly in water. These giants can easily crush a human being, although their usual prey is large animals. Many of the water inhabitants are huge. The manatee or sea cow is a mammal that breathes air through collapsible nostrils and suckles its live-born babies, but never leaves the rivers. A manatee eats only plants and is a docile creature. Measuring up to 7 feet (2 m) in length, manatees are probably the inspiration for the mermaid myths started by sailors hundreds of years ago.

Another river inhabitant is the capybara, or water pig (below). The world's largest rodent, it is the size of a small pig. It lives near water and can be found there for much of the day. Indigenous people hunt capybaras for their meat. The matamata *(MAH-tah-mah-tah) turtle lives in rivers and hunts fish by luring them with strange weedlike appendages on its head. A species of eel that carries 500 watts of electric current also inhabits Guyana's waterways.*

and Venezuela. These are dense forests that have largely escaped commercial logging because of their isolation. Some of the species that can be found there include greenheart, mora, and crabwood. These trees can grow up to hundreds of feet tall. Greenheart is especially valuable because its wood does not rot in seawater and can be used to build docks and wharves.

Notable smaller plants include hundreds of varieties of orchids, some of which have adapted to living in trees with no soil, and the Regis water lily, which lives in freshwater pools. This water lily, which can grow 6 feet (1.82 m) in diameter, is the largest leafed aquatic plant in the world. In the tropical jungle are several types of vines that live suspended from huge trees. The best known of these is the liana vine, a weak tree that grows up the trunk of another in search of sunlight. The bark of a different vine, known locally as *urari* (oo-RAH-ree), is used to make a poison that is more deadly than that of many snakes.

As a tropical country, Guyana also has many insects, including beautiful jungle butterflies, such as the Morpho butterfly, and leaf-cutter ants. The leaf-cutter or parasol ant is a species that grows a type of fungus for food in its underground nests. The fungus needs rotting vegetation to survive, so the leaf-cutters work hard to provide their food with food. They can strip a tree of leaves very quickly.

With so many rivers, it is no surprise that Guyana has an abundance of freshwater fish. Perhaps the most famous Amazon fish is the piranha, with its sharp teeth and carnivorous habits. Some species of piranha attack humans and other large mammals, but most are not meat-eaters. They prefer still pools of water, so many rapids and waterfalls in Guyana are safe. A favorite with sport fishermen is the *lukanani* (loo-kah-NAH-nee), which resembles the large mouth bass. Another member of Guyana's diverse fish life is the arapaima, which can weigh up to 200 pounds (91 kg).

Bird life includes dozens of species of hummingbirds with beautiful plumage and a wide array of parrots and macaws. An illusive jungle dweller is the golden Cock-of-the-Rock (*Rupicola rupicola*). The males are a golden-orange color with a crest that looks like like a Roman helmet. They have an unusual mating ritual, where the male bird clears an area of jungle floor and strikes a variety of poses while waiting for the brown-colored female to choose from among the competitors. Some males wait for weeks and are never chosen.

HUMAN SETTLEMENTS

A residential development in Georgetown.

The most heavily populated region is the coast. About 90 percent of the Guyanese live and work there. The other three zones support scattered populations of mostly indigenous people who live off the land.

The capital city, Georgetown, has the largest urban population, at about 200,000. Located at the mouth of the Demerara River, the city was founded by the British in 1781. The Dutch later claimed the settlement, but it was finally won by the British and given its present name in 1812. Georgetown is one of the best examples of a Georgian-style wooden Caribbean city. Many of the colonial buildings have been preserved, as have the large tree-lined avenues built by the Dutch. Other important cities include Linden, 40 miles (64 km) south of Georgetown on the Demerara River, and New Amsterdam, 62 miles (99.77 km) southeast of Georgetown at the mouth of the Berbice River.

All three cities are important shipment points for Guyana's most valuable mineral, bauxite. Linden and New Amsterdam are considerably smaller than Georgetown, with populations of about 60,000 and 33,000, respectively. There are many other small settlements along the coast but very few inland.

HISTORY

A statue of Cuffy, who led a famous slave revolt in 1763, in Georgetown's Independence Square. Cuffy is revered as a national hero for his role in the fight for freedom.

G UYANA HAS AN INCREDIBLY diverse ethnic composition, which includes indigenous Amerindians and descendants of people from Africa, India, China, and Europe. This modern blend, representing all the major cultures of the world—Native American, European, Asian, and African—was not accidental, but is the result of historical events.

First the Dutch, and later the British, relied on the allegiance of Amerindians to help control the African slaves. Amerindians were used as militia, and friendly relations were maintained with them through trade until slavery was ended in 1834.

Thousands of supporters of the People's National Congress party (PNC) gathered to hear party leaders tell Britain and the world that they wanted independence in July 1965.

A sketch of precolonial life in Guyana shows early natives fishing on a dugout canoe along the Essequibo River.

Guyana had two different colonial masters before independence in 1966, and much of its history has been driven by the demands of these European powers and their desire to gain from their colonies. The aftermath of the colonial history continues to haunt modern Guyana through ethnic politics and discord.

THE PRECOLONIAL PERIOD

Before Europeans even suspected that the Americas existed, people were already living in the area that became Guyana. These indigenous inhabitants, known today as Amerindians, were largely seminomadic, living in stable settlements for a period of time before moving their villages to new locations. They mainly practiced shifting horticulture, growing staple crops such as cassava in small farm plots, and also hunting and fishing. Most villages consisted of one or two large extended families of fewer than 70 people.

These villages had no formal leaders or chiefs, but important men from each of the families competed to become informal village leaders. When this competition became heated, or when the village grew too large for the farms to support the people, some members moved out to form new settlements. Each village also had a shaman, whose job included curing the sick and maintaining good relations between the people and the spirits and gods. In the Guianas (including present-day Guyana, Suriname, and French Guiana), there were several different groups of people. When the first Europeans arrived, they encountered the Carib and Arawak near the coast and the Warrau and Akawáio farther inland.

EUROPEAN DISCOVERY AND EARLY RELATIONS

Since people were already living in Guyana, it is not quite accurate to talk about "discovery" by Europeans as if they were the first inhabitants. Christopher Columbus sailed by the coast of the Guianas on his third voyage in 1498, but did not land there due to the inhospitable appearance of the mangrove forests and swamps along the shore. It was not until nearly a hundred years later that the Dutch, who were then a major commercial power, and English explorers and settlers began to take an interest in the Guianas. The first explorers, the most notable being Sir Walter Raleigh, an English adventurer and writer, brought back stories that inspired both European powers to promote colonization.

Slaves working at a sugarcane plantation in the early days of colonialism.

The first permanent settlement was founded in 1616 on an island in the estuary of the Essequibo River. It was led by the Dutch but included English settlers as well. This colony expanded to the Demerara River later that century, and a separate Dutch colony was founded on the Berbice River. At first Europeans settled the riverbanks far inland and away from the coast. The economy of these early settlements was based on growing tropical crops such as tobacco, cotton, coffee, and cocoa, and on trade with local Amerindian groups for forest products such as annatto (a vegetable dye) and letter wood from trees. Unlike the Spanish and Portuguese who established settlements elsewhere on the South American continent, the Dutch maintained friendly relations with the Amerindians and did not use them as slaves.

PLANTATION SOCIETY

Throughout the second half of the 1600s, European settlers began to move toward the coast and away from their riverine farms. At the same time there was an economic shift from crops such as cotton and tobacco toward sugar.

RALEIGH'S VISION OF GUYANA

Sir Walter Raleigh, better known for his efforts to establish a colony in Virginia, also explored what later became Guyana. He made two voyages in 1595 and 1617 for Queen Elizabeth I of England, searching for the fabled El Dorado, or land of gold. This was a rumor started around the time of Christopher Columbus's early voyages that there existed a land of indigenous people whose capital city was called Manoa. Reportedly, the city and the people were covered with gold. Many adventures began in Europe with the idea of finding this legendary land, and Raleigh believed that it was located inland from the Guianese coast. Although he never found Manoa or El Dorado, his writings about his travels inspired many others to seek their fortunes in the Guianas.

For example, he told prospective explorers that they "shall find there more rich and beautiful cities, more temples adorned with golden images, than either Cortez found in Mexico, or Pizarro in Peru . . . , Guiana is a country that is still untouched . . . , the face of the earth is still untorn." In another passage he described a crystal mountain covered with diamonds where waters fall. The waterfall was described as making the sound of "1,000 great bells . . . , knocked one against the other." Years later exploration of the great sandstone plateaus such as Roraima confirmed the story. Waterfalls do indeed cascade over mountains and sometimes the light does make the sand particles of the rock shine like diamonds!

The first sugarcane plantation was started in 1658, and throughout the 1700s, the Essequibo and Demerara colonies became more and more dependent on this one crop. The Dutch set out to reclaim coastal swamplands and protected the reclaimed land from the sea by constructing walls and dikes. Once it was fortified, the land was planted with large estates of sugarcane. Hundreds of thousands of African slaves were brought in to work on sugarcane and cotton plantations in the Americas, and the Dutch plantations were among the worst in terms of the abuse of human rights. The appalling conditions of slavery sparked off many minor rebellions as well as a couple of major ones in Guyana. One slave revolt led by Cuffy in 1763 made him a national hero.

This memorial remembers the 1763 slave rebellion in Georgetown.

FIGHTING FOR CONTROL

Toward the end of the 18th century, control of the colonies at Essequibo, Demerara, and Berbice shifted several times between the British and the Dutch. The British first seized control of the three colonies in 1781. However, they only held on for a year before the French, allies of the Dutch, took back the colonies and returned them to Dutch control. In 1796 the British captured the colonies again and managed to hold on to them for six years. The Treaty of Amiens, signed in 1802, returned the colonies to the Dutch once again. This treaty held for only one year before the Netherlands and Britain once again went to war and the colonies returned to British control. All this flip-flopping ended in 1814, when the Dutch finally gave the colonies to Britain. Essequibo, Demerara, and Berbice were united in a single colony called British Guiana in 1831.

Sugar sustained colonial Guiana and continues to be an important product in the modern economy. The wealth that it generated, however, came at the expense of many thousands of lives lost or lived in poverty and misery, first in slavery and later under the indenture system.

The life of a slave began with capture in West Africa and shipment to the New World in ships designed to hold as many people as possible. If the slave survived this horrifying journey, called "the Middle Passage," he or she would be auctioned off at one of the slave ports in South or North America. From there began a life of misery. Slaves on Dutch estates were expected to work a minimum of 14 hours a day, starting at dawn. They had to work in the sugarcane fields and do any other chores required by the estate master. In addition, they were expected to grow some of their own food at night to supplement the meager rations provided by the owner. Any misbehavior was punishable by the whip and other inhumane tortures such as the amputation of a leg or death by burning over a slow fire. Not surprisingly many slaves tried to escape or revolt.

Indentured workers, most of them from India, were legally free, unlike slaves, but they also suffered inhumane working and living conditions. From the point at which they signed their contracts in their home countries, their rights were ignored. Contractors often lied about conditions in Guyana to attract workers and even resorted to kidnapping unwilling workers. They, too, were crowded onto ships under unsanitary conditions and left to fend for themselves during the long journey. Some ships had mortality rates of up to 25 percent. Indentured workers were supposed to work a 7- or 10-hour day, depending on whether they were in the fields or the factory, but in reality they often worked 11 to 18 hours a day. This was hardly any improvement over slavery.

Workers were fined for resisting the system and sometimes beaten and whipped, just as the slaves had been. They received no legal protection from the colonial state and were often arrested or killed when they "rebelled" in an attempt to get justice.

Sugar has much to answer for in the history of Guyana since it forms such a tragic part of the history of both the Afro- and Indo-Guyanese.

THE 19TH CENTURY

The most significant event in Guyana's history during the 19th century was the emancipation of the African slaves. British Guiana was then one of the main producers of sugar in the Caribbean region. When the slaves were given their freedom in 1834, many of them decided to leave the estates and work plots of their own land in the towns, and they became the majority urban population. This created a severe labor shortage on the estates, and plantation owners lobbied the British government to find a solution to their problem.

The solution was the indentured labor system. The indenture system worked by contracting laborers in their home countries for a fixed period of work—usually five to seven years—in return for their passage to the country where they would work and either their passage home at the end or the option to stay on in their new country. Wages were fixed and very low, which allowed the plantation owners to continue to produce sugar at competitive prices. Although indentured workers were formally free, the conditions of work were not much of an improvement over slavery.

An artist's impression of Georgetown in 1888.

A United Nations tribunal in 2007 ruled in the century-old dispute between Guyana and Suriname over maritime territory, giving both a share of a potentially oil-rich offshore basin.

The first group of laborers brought to Guyana under contract to work for the plantations included the English, Irish, and Germans. This trial lasted only from 1835 to 1839 because northern Europeans were too susceptible to tropical diseases. One group, however, proved to be quite adaptable—the Portuguese. For 27 years, from 1835 to 1862, a total of 31,628 Portuguese workers were brought to British Guiana. When their contracts ended, many stayed on and entered small commercial enterprises. To meet the heavy demand for labor, other countries were targeted by the indenture system— India and China.

Chinese indentured laborers began to arrive in 1853. By 1912 this flow of labor was halted, but by then about 14,000 workers had come to British Guiana and many, like the Portuguese, stayed on and entered commercial trades. But by far the biggest group of workers to be imported were the East Indians. The first workers arrived in 1838. By the time the practice was stopped due to a request from the colonial government in India in 1917, about 238,960 Indians had been transported to British Guiana. They formed the backbone of plantation labor during the 19th century and went on to become the majority ethnic group in modern Guyana. At the end of their work terms, some Indians decided to return home, and 75,547 people were repatriated between 1843 and 1949. Many others stayed on at the estates, and some gave up their right to return passage in order to receive parcels of land and become farmers in their new home. They developed rice agriculture in Guyana and are still the largest ethnic group in rural villages. The indenture system helped ease the labor shortage, but sugar production never recovered after the slaves were freed. Many small plantations could no longer compete and were bought out by bankers and other plantation owners. The result of this process set the stage for colonial politics in the 20th century.

PRE-INDEPENDENCE

British Guiana entered the 20th century with an 18th-century form of the colonial government that had been established by the Dutch. The country was effectively controlled by estate owners rather than by the people. In 1928 Britain reformed the system, abolishing the Dutch-established councils and

BOOKER'S GUIANA

At the time of emancipation in 1834, there were 308 sugarcane estates. By 1904, 66 years later, there were only 46 sugarcane estates. By 1967 there were just 18, and 15 of these sugarcane estates were controlled by a single company—the Booker Brothers Company.

Emancipation meant that sugarcane plantation owners no longer had free labor. Although indentured labor was successfully used, it cost more, and the change from one system to the other forced many smaller plantations out of business. At the same time people buying sugar in Britain were unhappy about having to pay more for Caribbean sugar in order to protect the plantations there. By 1836 the British government had decided to allow free competition between Caribbean planters and those in India. This also helped cause the failure and collapse of small estates. Two London-based companies that specialized in the sugar trade were Booker Brothers and John McConnell Company. Both companies benefited when the price of sugar fell in the 1880s; they were able to buy up estates that were no longer profitable.

In 1900 the two companies merged to form the Booker Brothers McConnell Company Limited. This commercial giant continued to expand ownership of ever larger estates until it controlled nearly the whole sugar industry. Booker Brothers, as

it was known locally, also expanded into other parts of Guyana's economy. It owned a network of retail stores, the largest taxi service in the country, a pharmaceutical factory, and rum distilleries. It was involved in publishing, advertising, real estate, insurance, cattle ranching, and even owned its own shipping service.

Until independence in 1966 Booker Brothers was the effective power in British Guiana's economy, so much so that the colony was often called "Booker's Guiana."

Cheddi Jagan, newly elected as prime minister, arrives in New York for informal talks with President Kennedy in 1961.

replacing them with a legislative council. Nevertheless the first election for the legislative council, in which everyone who was 21 or older could vote, was not held until 1953. Meanwhile the general population had become increasingly active in resisting British rule and British companies. The first mass political party, the People's Progressive Party (PPP), was founded in 1950 by Dr. Cheddi Jagan, an East Indian dentist, and Forbes Burnham, a British-educated Afro-Guyanese lawyer. Distinctly left-wing, the PPP won the elections of 1953, but the British governor suspended the government, claiming that this was a communist insurgence.

Forbes Burnham then broke away to form the People's National Congress (PNC) in 1957. The PPP continued to win subsequent elections despite Britain's intervention, and relations in the colony continued to worsen as numerous labor strikes were violently suppressed by the authorities. Before the 1964 elections, Britain changed the voting rules so that the PPP could not win a majority. Although the PNC also failed to gain a majority, it was able to form a coalition government with the United Force (UF) that largely represented Amerindian and Portuguese interests. Secure that the left-wing PPP was shut out of power, Britain granted Guyana its freedom in 1966.

GUYANA AFTER 1966

On gaining power in the newly independent country, Forbes Burnham set out to create a virtual dictatorship with himself and his party at the helm. In 1970 he proclaimed Guyana a cooperative republic and committed the country to a socialist economic path. In the early 1970s many foreign companies and industries were nationalized as part of this plan.

In 1980 Burnham approved a new constitution that gave the president more power. This constitution also guaranteed the right to work and affirmed the equality of women. The economy was suffering from low prices for its main exports, and there were food shortages and labor unrest. Burnham cracked down on the people and was accused by local and international organizations of rigging the 1980 elections that put him in power once again. Burnham died in August 1985 and was succeeded by Vice President Hugh Desmond Hoyte.

Hoyte led the PNC to victory in the 1985 elections and reversed some of Burnham's policies during his term of office. In 1988 he began to work with the International Monetary Fund (IMF) to renovate Guyana's economy. These changes were part of his Economic Recovery Program (ERP) designed to increase private ownership of businesses and to encourage foreign investment in Guyana. Since the 1985 elections were also questionable, Hoyte agreed to electoral reform and to have international observers, such as the Carter Center of Atlanta, present for the next round of elections. To allow enough time to make necessary changes, elections were postponed from 1990 to 1992.

Much to the dismay of the PNC, Cheddi Jagan and the PPP won the 1992 elections. Jagan set out to revise the constitution to guarantee free elections in the future. He also committed his government to Hoyte's ERP, despite the high cost being paid by Guyana's workers and poor. When Jagan died in March 1997, Vice President Samuel A. Hinds became president until elections in December the same year. The PPP won the elections under their new leader, Janet Jagan, the late Cheddi Jagan's wife.

Since independence Guyana has struggled with a failing economy and political problems. First under Burnham's dictatorship and then under the harsh economic policies of the ERP, the Guyanese have seen both their civil liberties and ability to make a living deteriorate. This has caused massive immigration to countries such as the United States, Canada, Great Britain, and other countries in the Caribbean. The economy began to turn around in 1991, but by then, many educated Guyanese had already established new homes elsewhere. Guyana is one of the poorest countries in the Western Hemisphere, and it faces a major challenge to modernize its economy and improve human rights.

Forbes Burnham was a dominant figure in Guyanese politics for three decades until his death in 1985.

GOVERNMENT

The Gothic-style city hall in Georgetown.

INCE INDEPENDENCE FROM British rule, Guyana has seen several significant changes to its constitution and to the way in which representatives are elected to the government. Guyanese politics is largely based on party allegiance.

There are seven political parties, but only two have been dominant in running the country. Guyana holds membership in many international organizations and maintains good diplomatic relations with most of the world.

The seat of Guyana's parliament in Georgetown.

GOVERNMENT STRUCTURE

Local government is administered by the regional councils, whose members are also elected for five-year terms. They can be dissolved by the president before the end of their term. Large cities, such as Georgetown, have elected city councils as well.

On February 23, 1970, four years after Guyana gained independence from the British, Forbes Burnham, who was then the elected prime minister, turned Guyana into a cooperative republic within the Commonwealth of Nations—a group of countries that includes Great Britain and its former colonies. Burnham remained in power throughout the 1970s, during which time he designed a new constitution. The new constitution took effect on October 6, 1980, and has undergone several amendments.

Guyana's government consists of the office of the president and the elected unicameral National Assembly, which has 65 members. Out of 65 members, 40 are elected directly by proportional representation (PR) at the national level. The other 25 are elected by PR at the regional level—in other words, each region elects a certain number of representatives to parliament. The president appoints a vice president and prime minister (both titles apply to the same person) from among the elected members of the assembly. The president is the supreme executive authority, head of state, and commander of the armed forces, and is elected for a five-year term. This term can be extended by the president for a period of one year up to five times in a row, so that ten years may pass between elections. There is no limit to the number of terms that the same person may serve as president of the country.

Guyana is not divided into electoral districts. The whole country is considered a single electing body, and anyone who is at least 18 years of age, has Guyanese citizenship, and lives in the country on election day is eligible to vote. For all the elected seats in the National Assembly, people vote for a party rather than for an individual. The party that wins the largest number of seats forms the government.

There are ten regions in Guyana, each of which has a Regional Development Council with 12 to 35 elected members. Each of these councils elects one of its members to serve in the National Assembly. Two members from each regional council also serve in the National Congress of Democratic Organs. This 20-member congress then elects two of its members to complete the available seats in the National Assembly. Thus 53 seats are directly elected, whereas 12 are indirectly elected through regional councils.

The flag of Guyana, which was adopted in 1966, has a green background with a white-bordered yellow triangle from side to side, superimposed with a black-bordered red triangle half the size of the yellow one. All the colors have significance for the country and its people. Red represents the people's energy in building a new country, while black represents perseverance. Mineral wealth and the country's forward thrust are represented by yellow and its rivers by white. Green represents the economic resources of agriculture and forests. The white border symbolizes the rivers.

The coat of arms was also adopted in 1966 and includes symbols that represent people, nature, and history: an Amerindian headdress representing the indigenous people of the country; two diamonds representing mining; a helmet representing the monarchy (of Great Britain); a shield decorated with the national flower, the Regis water lily; two jaguars holding a pickax, sugarcane, and rice to symbolize labor and the main agricultural industries; three wavy blue lines representing Guyana's many waterways; and a Canje pheasant representing the national bird.

The motto of the country is "One People, One Nation, One Destiny."

In addition to these elected members, nonelected Guyanese may also play important roles in government. The speaker of the house, for example, is chosen by the assembly on the first day of a new government, but may not be one of the elected representatives. If the speaker is chosen from outside, he or she loses the power to cast tie-breaking votes. The president can also choose additional vice presidents, ministers, and members of his cabinet from outside the group of elected representatives. These people become part of the government, but they do not vote in the National Assembly. The president also chooses the leader of the opposition from among the elected representatives.

To vote a bill into law, one-third of the assembly must be present, and the majority must agree. The approved bill then passes to the president. If the president chooses, he or she may reject the bill and send it back to the assembly for revision. The assembly can then change the bill according to presidential instructions or, with a two-thirds majority, send the bill back to the president for approval. In such a case, the president must sign the bill into law within 21 days or dissolve the assembly. In the case of dissolution, elections must be called immediately. Although the president of Guyana is powerful, he or she cannot veto a bill approved by the majority of the National Assembly.

Children wave election signs for Guyanese president Bharrat Jagdeo during a closing rally celebration in Georgetown during the 2001 elections.

POLITICAL PARTIES

Guyana has more than ten registered political parties, but only two have ever formed the government. Two others have also held small numbers of seats in various governments, but have never formed the opposition. The two dominant parties are the PPP and the PNC.

The PPP was the first party ever established in Guyana and was founded in 1950 by Dr. Cheddi Jagan. A few years later, after disagreements among party leaders, Forbes Burnham left the PPP and founded the PNC in 1957. The UF is a small right-wing party that has generally sided with the PNC. The Working People's Alliance (WPA) began as a group promoting the rights of workers. In 1979 the group declared itself a political party. It has a left-wing, collective leadership. For the 1992 elections, Cheddi Jagan organized a coalition of left-wing opposition parties that campaigned to end electoral malpractice. This group called itself the Patriotic Coalition for Democracy (PCD) and included the PPP, WPA, Democratic Labor Movement, and the People's Democratic Movement.

THE JUDICIARY

The Supreme Court of Judicature in Guyana consists of the Court of Appeal, the High Court, and a number of courts of Summary Jurisdiction. The High Court has jurisdiction over all civil matters that are referred to it by local magistrates. It has limited powers in criminal matters. Appeals are taken to either the Court of Appeal or the High Court, with right of final appeal to the Caribbean Court of Justice. The chief justice is head of the High Court and is a member of the Court of Appeal.

Guyana's High Court in Georgetown.

THE MILITARY

The Guyana Defense Force (GDF) has about 80,000 members. It has its origin in the Special Service Unit (SSU), which started under the British as an internal security force. Under Burnham the SSU was converted to Guyana's army, navy, and air force, and leadership was given to black officers. In this way the GDF was used more to contain resistance to Burnham's dictatorship than to protect Guyana's borders.

The Guyana Police Force is similarly predominantly black and was also used by Burnham to protect his position. A paramilitary force called the Guyana National Service (GNS), which was made up of young people about to enter college, was dissolved by President Bharrat Jagdeo's administration. Instead of serving one year of national service in remote areas of the country before beginning their studies, they are being trained in entrepreneurial skills to become businesspeople. The 1990s saw positive changes in free elections and a shift away from PNC power. Fortunately the military and paramilitary accepted these changes.

GUYANA'S FIRST WOMAN PRESIDENT

Janet Jagan was elected president of Guyana on December 19, 1997, with 54 percent of the votes. She replaced her deceased husband, Dr. Cheddi Jagan, as leader of the PPP. American-born, she met Dr. Jagan when he was studying dentistry in the United States in the early 1940s. They married in the United States and returned to Guyana in 1943. She always shared his political interests. In August 1999 she announced her resignation due to ill health and named Finance Minister Bharrat Jagdeo as her successor until new elections were held in 2001. Since then, Jagdeo has won two elections, in 2001 and 2006, and is currently the president of Guyana.

FOREIGN RELATIONS

Guyana enjoys cordial relations with most other countries. Some concerns have plagued relations with neighbors, however. Both Venezuela and Suriname have, at different times, claimed land within Guyana's borders as their own. At one point diplomatic relations with Suriname were completely severed. These were restored in 1979, but Guyana still protests that Surinamese maps include a part of its territory in the southeast. The dispute with Venezuela goes back to the colonial times. Although neither party has agreed to let the matter drop, conflict has been confined to the diplomatic level. Since gaining independence in 1966, Guyana has maintained diplomatic relations with many nations. Guyana holds membership with the European Union (EU), the Caribbean Community and Common Market (CARICOM), the Inter-American Development Bank (IDB), the UN Development Program (UNDP), the World Health Organization (WHO), the United Nations Children's Fund (UNICEF), the World Bank, and the International Monetary Fund (IMF).

Bharrat Jagdeo is the current president of Guyana.

GUYANA VERSUS VENEZUELA

The region claimed by both Guyana and Venezuela is the eastern section of the Guiana Highlands, of which Mount Roraima is a part. This geological formation contains minerals such as bauxite, nickel, and manganese; iron, diamonds, and gold, and this wealth is the reason both parties have persevered for so long. Constituting about three-fifths of Guyana's current territory, the disputed area involves land west of the Essequibo River.

The dispute started in the 19th century when the British claimed the territory for themselves. Venezuela had controlled it, but lost control when its outposts were closed due to civil war in the early 1800s. The British sent in an expedition to mark the border in 1844 and, from that point on, Venezuela disputed the new international border. Venezuela asked the British to agree to abide by the decision of an international tribunal, but until the United States became involved in the 1890s, the British refused. Finally bowing to international pressure, the British agreed to the tribunal. The tribunal's decision, which favored the British claim, was issued on October 3, 1899, in Paris, in an agreement since known as the Paris Tribunal. Everything seemed to be settled until 1944, when one of the members of the tribunal died, leaving behind a confidential document arguing that the tribunal had been biased in favor of the British. Once again matters heated up.

When Guyana gained its independence, the new government, along with the British and the Venezuelans, committed itself to trying to find a peaceful settlement. Venezuela ignored this agreement when it occupied Ankoko Island in 1966. By 1970, in order to avoid making the crisis worse, Venezuela and Guyana agreed to do nothing further for 12 years in a document known as the Port of Spain Protocol. When this period expired in 1982, the Venezuelans refused to renew it, thus opening talks once again. At this point the matter was referred to the United Nations (UN) for settlement. To date there has been no UN proposal, and the leaders of the two countries, as well as the UN-appointed consultant, continue to meet regularly to discuss the issue. Hoyte visited two different Venezuelan presidents in 1987 and 1989, Dr. Jagan went in 1993, and Janet Jagan paid a visit to President Rafael Caldera in July 1998. Relations have improved considerably since the tense 1960s, but neither side has conceded its claim."

ECONOMY

Sacks of sugar being kept in a warehouse.

CHAPTER 4

GUYANA FACES UNIQUE ECONOMIC problems and challenges due to its small size, limited resources, and colonial heritage. Since independence the various governments have tried two radically different strategies to improve the standard of living for the Guyanese.

Both have resulted in impoverishment for different reasons. Although the future looks brighter now than it has for many years, the people continue to struggle to make ends meet in this very poor country.

TWO PATHS TO DEVELOPMENT

From 1970 on Burnham instituted a number of major economic reforms, changing the British system. He renamed Guyana a cooperative republic. His goal was to create a socialist economy in which major industries were owned and run on a cooperative basis. This meant that there could be no foreign ownership, so Burnham set out to nationalize the country's main foreign-controlled companies. The biggest were the Booker Brothers' sugar interests,

Workers packaging noodles at a local factory.

A worker in the Demerara Province piles sugarcane on barges for transportation.

the Demerara Bauxite Company (owned by Canada's ALCAN), and American-owned Reynolds Mines (also a bauxite mining interest). Besides sugar and bauxite, Burnham also created a number of government-owned enterprises to produce or manage every other aspect of the economy and nationalized 29 other companies.

By 1975 Guyana was facing economic difficulty when the prices for both bauxite and sugar declined on the world market. Burnham borrowed money to keep the economy going, but this only increased Guyana's foreign debt. Inflation ballooned, and by 1989, four years after Burnham's death, Guyana had replaced Haiti as the poorest country in the Western Hemisphere.

After coming into office as Burnham's successor, Desmond Hoyte began to negotiate with international agencies such as the IMF to restructure the economy and renegotiate the country's debt. In 1988 Hoyte introduced the ERP, which reversed Burnham's policies. Under the ERP, Guyana began to encourage foreign investment and sold some government companies to private owners. For example, a new bauxite mine was opened in Aroima with Reynolds, and a gold mine concession on the Omai River was granted to foreign companies. Sugarcane land was not sold back to Booker, but Booker Tate, the successor to Booker Brothers McConnell, was hired to oversee sugar production in order to boost output.

One of the demands of the IMF was that the government had to reduce expenses. As a result many government workers lost their jobs. In one bauxite mine alone, 700 out of 3,000 workers were laid off between 1992 and 1994, and there were plans to let another 1,100 workers go in the future. Guyana was also forced to allow its currency, the Guyana dollar, to "float"—that is, let it reflect the true strength of the Guyanese economy on the world market. Effectively a devaluation of the currency occurred; more and more dollars were needed to buy the same amount of foreign goods. Many of the world's poorer and indebted nations have had to go through these changes, which are called "structural adjustment." Although structural adjustment improves

ALL THAT IS GOLD DOES NOT GLITTER

The Omai Gold Mine began production in 1993 on the Omai River, a tributary of the Essequibo. It is jointly owned by a Canadian company, an American company, and the Guyanese government. The deposit was believed to hold an estimated 3.6 million ounces (1,020,584 kg) of gold, and the plan was to mine it over 10 years. The mine is an open-pit mine, in which large holes are dug in the earth to get at the rocks containing gold. Once the rocks are crushed, a process called cyanide leaching separates out the gold. As the name implies, cyanide, a highly toxic poison, is the main chemical used in this process. It evaporates quickly, but long-term exposure to even low levels of cyanide can cause mental retardation.

In August 1995 a waste pond collapsed, leaking 4.2 million cubic yards (3.2 million cubic m) of cyanide-contaminated waste into the river. People reported seeing fish and animals floating dead in the river far downstream. The Omai mine was closed for six months while American and Canadian experts conducted an investigation. Although these mining firms had been involved in prior incidences due to poor quality equipment and construction, no action was taken against them. They agreed to pay US$10 million in damages and resumed production in 1996 with no modifications to their mining practices. Close to the original estimate, approximately 3.8 million ounces (1,077,283 kg) of gold were produced from operations in 2005.

Exotic woods belong loaded onto a carrier along the Demerara River in Georgetown.

production, exports, and the government's ability to pay its debts, it does not improve the lives of the people. The Guyanese saw their standard of living plummet, as a result of high unemployment and inflation. This prompted massive immigration in the late 1980s and early 1990s.

MAIN INDUSTRIES

AGRICULTURE Agriculture is the biggest sector of the economy. The narrow coastal zone supports the two main export crops, sugarcane and rice, which together account for about 90 percent of all Guyana's agricultural exports. Sugar is still produced on large estates using manual labor. Because of the clay-based soil, machines cannot easily be used in Guyana. Instead the fields must be fertilized, planted, and cut by hand. This is grueling work in the hot sun and employs 20,000 workers. Because sugarcane is a seasonal product, not all of these people have work all year long.

Rice is the second most important agricultural product. Unlike sugar it is grown on relatively small family plots of 10 to 20 acres (4 to 8 ha). East Indian laborers began to grow rice when they finished their labor contracts in the 19th and 20th centuries. Today they still make up the majority of rice farmers, who number about 10,000 farm families. Other agricultural crops include coconuts, oranges, bananas, and plantains. Much of the land in the savannahs is used for cattle ranching, since it is not fertile enough for agriculture.

FORESTRY AND FISHING Tropical rain forest covers about three-quarters of Guyana, but until the 1990s it was underexploited, although there has always been some harvesting of trees, especially valuable hardwoods.

In 1991 the government gave out the largest timber concession ever to a foreign company to produce plywood in a Georgetown factory. Plywood exports to the United States quadrupled as a result of this deal. Shrimp fishing in the ocean is the main focus of the commercial fishing industry. American and Japanese companies control much of this industry.

A worker checks up on the production of Demerara sugar, which is all processed from sugarcane plants,

MINING Bauxite (used for producing aluminum) and gold together represented some 40 percent of Guyana's exports in 2005. Bauxite mining started in Guyana in 1916, with the biggest mine in Linden and a second mine in the Berbice River region. Bauxite can be processed to produce calcium carbonate and alumina, which is the key component in aluminum. Although bauxite is a valuable export, it does not require large numbers of workers, since machines can do much of the work. It is also subject to large price fluctuations, which makes the exporting country vulnerable to economic ups and downs. In addition, more and more developed countries are now recycling aluminum, thus reducing demand and pushing down prices. Nevertheless, with the new mine in Aroima, Guyana will continue to mine bauxite and be dependent on the money it brings to the economy. Gold has been mined on a small-scale basis for many years, but only in 1993 did the government grant a large concession to a foreign firm. Since then gold revenues have grown and made a significant contribution to export earnings, though the mine does not employ a large number of people. In 2005 Guyana produced about 1.4 million tons (metric) of bauxite, 391,611 ounces (11,102 kg) of gold, and 340,000 carats (68 kg) of diamonds.

MANUFACTURING As well as growing and extracting raw materials, Guyana also processes these materials and produces manufactured goods, such as clothing, rum, and food. This sector of the economy accounts for 21 percent of the value of domestic production.

THE WORKFORCE

Guyana's labor force totals about 281,300 (2008 estimate) people. Industry and commerce employ about 102,000; agriculture employs 85,000; and the service industry employs about 85,000 people.

About 11 percent of the population is unemployed, and the rest are engaged in activities not clearly defined. Two trends are evident in employment—the rising unemployment over the last 30 years and the growing number of women in the labor force. Both trends reflect the weak economy and the effects of the ERP inaugurated in 1988, which has forced more people out of work.

Workers unload cargo in Georgetown's port.

TRADE

Guyana's main trading partners for exports in 2008 were the Canada, United States, United Kingdom, Ukraine, the Netherlands, Jamaica, Germany, and Trinidad and Tobago. Its chief imports are fuel and lubricants, heavy equipment, and manufactured consumer goods such as appliances. Guyana mainly imports from CARICOM countries, United States, Trinidad and Tobago, Venezuela, European Union, China, the Netherlands, Antilles-Curaco, Japan, and Suriname.

TRANSPORTATION

In the coastal zone, there are more than 367 miles (590 km) of paved and good-weather roads linking towns and villages. There are highways linking Linden and Georgetown that serve the mining and forestry sectors, and

In 1967 Guyana became one of the signatories to the Caribbean Free Trade Area, which later became CARICOM in 1973. Members of CARICOM include all the former British colonies in the Caribbean Basin. The Secretariat of CARICOM is located in Georgetown. In 1991 CARICOM signed a trade cooperation agreement with the United States, the first step for the Caribbean countries to become part of the American plan to unite the whole Western Hemisphere in a single trade agreement.

This would eventually mean that all products produced anywhere in North, Central, or South America, or the Caribbean would be available to consumers in the entire region with no extra taxes. Currently many countries protect their producers with special taxes on imports. Smaller economies such as Guyana's are concerned about competing with giants such as the United States and Canada, but free trade would give all the Americas an advantage in competition with other trading blocs such as the European Union. CARICOM is the first step along this path for Guyana.

another links Linden with Lethem, on the Brazilian border. There are no public railways in the country, although two small private lines operate to transport minerals from the mines to the ports. Most people living in the interior of the country are either completely isolated from the coast or travel by air to make the journey over dense forests. Depending on the point of origin and the destination, river travel is also common, as there are some 3,666 miles (5,900 km) of navigable rivers. The Berbice, Demerara, and Essequibo rivers are navigable by oceangoing vessels for 93 miles (150 km), 62 miles (100 km), and 49 miles (79 km), respectively.

Guyana has a government-owned airline called Guyana Airways Corporation. It links the major settlements in the interior with the coast and has regular flights to destinations such as Canada and the United States leaving from Cheddi Jagan International Airport at Timehri, 25 miles (40 km) south of Georgetown. Guyana has two seaports. The older one is in Georgetown and was built to handle the transportation of sugar. The second is in New Amsterdam and was built primarily to ship bauxite and its derivatives. The three river ports are in Essequibo, Kaituma, and Linden.

ENVIRONMENT

Water lilies float serenely at the bank of Lake Capoey in Guyana.

CHAPTER 5

GUYANA IS A BEAUTIFUL LAND OF forests, rivers, waterfalls, and clean air. Human activities since colonial times have spoiled some of that beauty. The most affected areas are in the narrow coastal plain. Strips of swampy land were cleared to make way for agriculture and settlement. The huge hinterland remains largely unchanged except for forestry and mining activities in various locations.

Water is a gift and is essential for life. In this sense Guyana is blessed, earning it the enviable nickname "land of many waters." Guyana is crisscrossed with long rivers, more than 275 waterfalls, and 18 lakes.

The exotic-looking Hoatzin adult resting on its nest.

Guyana does not face threats of volcanoes, hurricanes, or earthquakes. The main threat stems from flooding from sea-level rise. People coming from large urban cities are surprised at how spacious the urban centers in the plains are, even in the capital city of Georgetown. Wide avenues, gardens, and trees adjoin wooden buildings that are no higher than a few floors. Sea breezes from the Atlantic Ocean cool this tropical country. Unfortunately the charm is tarnished by Guyana's twin environmental problems—water pollution and waste disposal.

For Guyana the need to eradicate poverty without compromising its largely pristine natural environment can be a challenge. Still Guyana's leaders and people look set to reverse the bad situations to make Guyana more attractive.

A new construction in the middle of the rain forest.

CAUSES AND EFFECTS OF POLLUTION

MINING IMPACTS Guyana is rich in minerals. Gold, diamonds, bauxite, and granite are the targets of the mining sector. Kaolin, copper, lead, zinc, tungsten, nickel, iron, uranium, amethyst, green quartz, agate, jasper, and petroleum are also in demand. Small-scale miners pan for gold along rivers and creeks. Established miners dredge large sections of land or waterways. The mining sector depends on the demand for the type of minerals.

Mining in Guyana attracts foreign investments, which in turn creates jobs for many Guyanese people. However, the methods of extraction have negative impacts on the natural environment. Rivers are filled with silt when hydraulic dredges are used to extract gold along the banks.

The use of chemicals in the extraction process is a major concern. For instance, caustic soda (sodium hydroxide) is used in bauxite production. To extract gold from hard rocks, mercury is used, with cyanide as a by-product. There have been reports of illness caused by the use of creek or river water in mining districts. Chemicals may have been carelessly released into the water, contaminating it.

Mining works being carried out in a rain forest in Guyana. Tons of forest land are cleared each year to make room for economic development.

Loss of villages and natural wildlife habitats is another issue associated with the mining sector. Soil erosion takes place when vegetation is cleared. This results in landslides during heavy storms.

LOGGING DEBRIS Guyana's most precious asset is the rain forests; over 80 percent of Guyana is covered by rain forest. The forestry sector is necessary for Guyana's economic growth. However, the methods used for logging are sometimes not sustainable. Debris in the streams and rivers pollutes the water. Mangroves and the natural habitats of marine life are destroyed or threatened. Logging activities also affect water channels through siltation of the water. Sediments from logging operations cloud the rivers.

Another potential hazard is sawmill waste. It raises biochemical oxygen demand, jeopardizing aquatic lives in the rivers. At the sawmills, rough sawn lumber is treated with chemicals to prevent attack from fungi and insects. Careless handling of chemicals can lead to poisoning of rivers and streams.

Untreated sewage being pumped into the ocean in Georgetown. This, along with other types of agricultural and industrial waste, is harmful to marine life.

AGRICULTURAL POLLUTANTS In a land of many rivers and springs, there is enough water for public use, agriculture, and industrial needs. Much of the water pollution on Guyana's coast is caused by the agricultural industry. The most prevalent agricultural pollutants are synthetic fertilizers that contain nitrate. In Guyana rice is cultivated twice a year, of which about five months are spent using fertilizers to promote the growth of crops or pesticides to control bugs. Little consideration is given to runoff that hurts the ecosystem of both plants and fish.

Spillage is caused by careless handling of chemicals by laborers. Pesticides are used to control weeds in the coastal canals. They similarly impact the aquatic ecosystem as a whole. Laboratory and field testing of water, soil, plants, and animal samples in 2009 found that aquatic water bodies were contaminated by agricultural pollutants.

CLIMATE CHANGE IMPACTS ON MARINE LIFE

Baby leatherback turtles will wait until dusk to emerge and head for the sea.

Over the last decade the immediate impact of climate change has resulted in a temperature rise of 0.1°C (32°F) in Latin America and the Caribbean. Sea-level rise on the Atlantic has changed the nesting patterns of turtles on the beaches of Guyana. The beaches in Guyana have been the nesting place of turtles for many years. In recent times locals have noticed changing nesting patterns. Turtles usually nest from March to August, but for the past few years the pattern has changed from mid-January to mid-July. Erosion of the beaches, which occurs naturally every 30 to 35 years, may be a contributing factor. Due to climate change, erosion is occurring before this cycle is up, and could happen within weeks.

Other impacts of climate change on sea turtles are due to increased ocean temperatures. This affects not only nesting habits but also feeding habits. At the World Wildlife Fund Sea Turtle Symposium (2006), the Guyana Marine Turtle Conservation Society learned that the nesting of olive ridleys, one of two main nesting turtles of Guyana, also an endangered species, has increased in French Guiana and Brazil. This may explain why Guyana has not been seeing many nestings of this species on its shores in recent years. These adverse impacts are expected to continue unless climate change is slowed down.

Fish stock is already depleting from overharvesting. With climate change affecting the temperature of the ocean and rising sea levels, plankton, which generates the food chain for marine life, will be further reduced. Guyana's low-carbon development strategy includes giving fish stocks a chance to rebuild and sustain themselves.

A suckermouth armored catfish lying on the river bottom near a fisherman in the Potaro River.

DEFORESTATION

LOSS OF MANGROVE FORESTS Guyana's forests remain in their pristine state today, but the swampy mangrove forests along the coast and Essequibo riverbanks had long been cleared by colonists to make way for the cultivation of crops. As a result several species of mangrove and indigenous trees are extinct now. In their places patches of paddy fields and sugarcane plantations are present.

What happens when the mangrove population decreases? The coast's natural defense against the Atlantic Ocean is lowered. The seawall prevents the homes, the sugarcane plantations, and rice fields from flooding each year. That wall cannot spare Guyana from the effects of climate change. In 2005 a massive flood devastated the coastal belt so much that the country faced a loss equivalent to 60 percent of its gross domestic product (GDP). This is because 90 percent of the population lives on this coast, which is already 3 feet (1 meter) below sea level.

Tropical rain forests such as these are homes to numerous species of plant, land, and marine life.

LOSS OF HARDWOODS When it comes to forest harvesting, many locals believe their forests are inexhaustible. The often-heard boast "Dah wood kyan done, Man," meaning "the forest is inexhaustible," is common among loggers, both legal and illegal. Logging for timber can affect many species of hardwoods. Some of these species, such as the greenheart and purpleheart, are indigenous to Guyana. The current rate of harvesting for timber is unsustainable. It takes many decades to grow a canopy of trees, but these are felled in a matter of hours using an electric chainsaw.

NATIONAL PARKS AND RESERVES Traditionally the indigenous Amerindians of Guyana have been the keepers of forestlands, and they have done an excellent job protecting the forests utilizing sustainable methods for their livelihood. With help from the government and rain forest conservation agencies, the Amerindians are able to reduce further damages to the forests and the ecosystem.

Tropical rains at Kaieteur National Park.

The Kaieteur National Park is one example of conservation. Located within one of the largest and most biodiverse rain forests in the world, the park covers 28,950 square miles (74,980 square km) of mountain range and lies between the Amazon and the Orinoco rivers. Within Kaieteur are about 20,000 different plant species of which 35 percent are endemic, making it one of the three richest tropical wilderness areas on Earth. In addition, the park has a low human population density consisting mainly of Amerindian villages. Kaieteur is therefore one of the few places on Earth where all options for conservation are available.

It is a good thing that the government of Guyana is committed to keeping Guyana's forests standing. The low-carbon economic development strategy of 2009 targets an economy approach based on conservation and sustainable harvesting. It focuses on using the tropical forests to remove atmostpheric carbon dioxide and slowing the rate of climate change.

Another conservation effort is the Iwokrama Project. The Iwokrama International Center for Rainforest Conservation and Development (IIC)—a rain forest conservation charity—was established by Guyana and the Commonwealth. The IIC shows how tropical forests can be conserved and sustainably used for ecological, social, and economic benefits to local, national, and international communities.

WILDLIFE PROTECTION

Given Guyana's lush tropical forests, savannahs, and low human population, the wildlife population should thrive. Still more than 30 animals such as the jaguar, leatherback turtle, harpy eagle, giant otter, caiman, and manatee are on the Red List for endangered species of the International Union for Conservation of Nature (IUCN). The Canje pheasant and the arapaima—the world's largest freshwater fish—are believed to be endangered, too. Mining, logging, settlement, and hunting have all contributed to this sad fate.

Guyana and Conservation International set up the Konashen Community-Owned Conservaton Area (COCA) to protect countless species of insects, arachnids, and other invertebrates. Many of these are still undiscovered and unnamed. The Konashen COCA provides a habitat for a remarkable diversity of amphibians, reptiles, birds, and mammals.

"Our deforestation rate is one of the lowest in the world and we want it to stay that way. However, we also face considerable development challenges. We need better schools and hospitals, more jobs and economic opportunities, and to meet all the other economic and social demands of Guyana's people."
–President Barrat Jagdeo

ECOTOURISM AND THE ENVIRONMENT

Guyana has little to offer on its 63 beaches to match the facilities available on nearby Caribbean islands. But all that is changing— Guyana's ecotourism industry has taken off and is growing. Endangered sea turtles, various flora and fauna, rivers, and rain forests are preserved in their natural state when tourists visit these sights. One can take a cruise down the Essequibo River in its natural rawness even as many of the world's rivers are being redistributed over agricultural lands or have dams built over them.

Tourists take in the sights at Orinduik Falls situated on the Guyana-Brazil border.

The Shell Beach Conservation Project serves as a haven to four of the eight endangered sea turtle species. The Botanical Gardens in Georgetown include 100 acres (40 ha) of plants and trees. The gardens are also home to endangered animals such as the manatee. Deeper in the forests, hundreds of birds such as the macaw, toucan, or harpy eagle can be spotted in the native habitats. Stranger animals and rarer ones can also be spotted. It is hoped that ecotourism will eventually replace mining and logging in economic value. Adventure tourism and nature tourism may not preserve the environment; ecotourism does it better.

WASTE TREATMENT AND DISPOSAL

A major environmental issue for Guyana is waste management, including waste disposal, land use, and drainage. Urban centers such as Georgetown, New Amsterdam, Linden, Lethem, and Anna Regina have solid waste issues. Being centers for commerce, industry, administration, and residential use, they face similar problems of high population density, land use conflict, and poor infrastructure related to waste disposal.

To have a healthy environment, progressive communities employ a strategy to sort, recycle, convert, and dispose of their garbage and waste. In

WASTE MANAGEMENT

A total of 50 percent of the pit latrines in Guyana are not considered improved sanitary facilities by the UNESCO/WHO. Sewers only exist in Georgetown and are managed by the Central Georgetown Sewerage System, which was set up 80 years ago. The government has revealed plans to modernize this system and upgrade other facilities to improve waste management. For solid waste management to enjoy long-term success, people must understand the importance of reducing, reusing, and recycling. Relevant agencies and groups on solid waste management have started conducting public awareness campaigns since 2006.

this respect, Guyana's solid waste management is far from adequate. Because Guyana's economy is concentrated in the narrow fertile coastal strip, towns and cities mushroomed to cater to the demands of the various industries. People here consume more processed food and packaged goods. Most waste in the past was biodegradable. The lack of resources and proper guidelines result in illegal garbage dumping, particularly of car tires and lumber yard waste. There is no proper landfill for final disposal of solid waste. The practice is to burn or dispose of waste in open-air dumping sites.

Another waste issue is sanitation. Without proper access to toilet facilities people are at risk for poor health. The 2008 World Water Symposium reported that 80 percent of all deaths globally are due to poor water and sanitation. Water is not a big issue in Guyana, but sanitation systems can be improved.

In a time frame of only a few decades, human consumption patterns have drastically changed the environment. People have increased their use of energy, raw materials, and land. They have also produced more waste and destroyed some ecosystems. In terms of preserving its rain forests and ecosystems, Guyana has done better than many rain forest countries. Guyana is party to several environmental agreements on biodiversity, climate change, desertification, endangered species, ozone-layer protection, and law of the sea.

It will take much courage and determination to resolve the current environmental issues that are faced by this country. Guyana's environment has not reached critical levels that warrant quick action. The nation's approach is one of prevention rather than response.

GUYANESE

Young Guyanese girls of mixed ethnicity.

G UYANA HAS A POPULATION OF 779,417 (2009 estimate). One of the many names for Guyana is "Land of Six Peoples." This refers to the main ethnic groups that formed the majority of the country's population during the colonial era—East Indian, African, Amerindian, Chinese, European (largely British), and the Portuguese, who were regarded as a separate group because they came as indentured laborers.

Colorfully dressed women of Indian ethnicity at a Hindu festival in Georgetown.

The Afro-Guyanese tend to live in towns, especially Georgetown. When slaves were finally freed in the 19th century, they quickly chose to distance themselves from plantation society. Many moved to urban areas and educated themselves to occupy better paying positions. From there, they expanded into the civil service and the bauxite industry. Today the Afro-Guyanese make up about 50 percent of the urban population.

Afro-Guyanese children,

All but one of these groups—the exception being the Amerindians—came to or were brought to Guyana because of sugar. As a result of the specific history of their arrival, different groups have come to occupy different niches in society.

ETHNIC GROUPS

Although the popular conception of Guyana is that it is composed of six groups—East Indian, African, Amerindian, Chinese, Portuguese, and other Europeans, the actual breakdown of the population is more complex, with a seventh important group—those of mixed African and European ancestry—included. Breakdown of the population by ethnicity cannot be precise in part because people sometimes identify themselves differently at different times and because census categories have changed over time. On the basis of the most recent estimates and figures available, the following percentages can be identified:

- Indo-Guyanese (people descended from East Indian immigrants): 43.5 percent
- Afro-Guyanese (people descended from African slaves and immigrants): 30.2 percent
- Mixed (people descended from African and European unions): 16.7 percent
- Amerindians (indigenous groups): 9.1 percent
- Others: 0.5 percent

The mixed group includes people with both African and European ancestors. Under slavery it was not uncommon for a white master to have children with his female slaves. Later, when indentured laborers arrived without wives of their own, they sometimes married women of African origin. The percentages above make clear that the two biggest groups are those of East Indian and African descent.

Portuguese and Chinese are also included in the "six" races, although their numbers are quite small. Whites, or those of European descent, are also a tiny minority. Amerindians represent a larger percentage of the population. Guyana is one of the few countries in the Americas where the number of original people has held steady or even increased in the 21st century.

Not only is the population as a whole complexly divided by ethnicity, but even within these larger categories there are differences and specificities.

INDO-GUYANESE People of East Indian descent make up the largest ethnic group. They can be divided into two subgroups—those who practice Hinduism and those who practice Islam as their religion. Unlike in India, where these differences have led to war and the separation of Pakistan and Bangladesh from India, the two subgroups of Indo-Guyanese live amicably in Guyana.

Islam-practicing Guyanese of East Indian descent at a restaurant in Georgetown.

Before the arrival of Europeans, most indigenous groups in the Amazon Basin and surrounding region relied on small-scale farming, hunting, and fishing. For this reason, they are usually classified first by language family rather than by distinct economic practices. Carib refers to a family of related languages rather than to one single language. Carib-speaking people are thought to have come from an area in the Amazon River valley, now in modern Brazil. They began to migrate northward around A.D. 1200, and by 1300 they were expanding into the Lesser Antilles (part of the islands of the Caribbean). There they intermarried with members of another language family, the Arawak. In this process Carib was lost, so that by the time Europeans encountered indigenous people on the islands, they spoke only Arawak languages. Carib speakers remained on the mainland in northern Venezuela, the Guianas, and parts of Brazil. Arawak speakers also inhabited parts of the mainland and were trying to expand along the northern coast of South America before European settlement. The third language group is Warrau. People of this group are found today between the Orinoco River in Venezuela and the Pomeroon River in Guyana. This is a swampy region, and it has been postulated that they moved here to escape the warlike Carib and Arawak speakers as the latter two groups expanded their territories.

AFRO-GUYANESE AND MIXED The descendants of African slaves and the mixture of these people with Europeans make up what is called Creole society. Although the slaves came from many different cultural groups in West Africa, they have lost most of the cultural and linguistic characteristics that separated them. This is a very common process wherever slaves were brought to live and is the result of the conditions of slavery in which the slaves were not allowed to maintain cultural differences among themselves. The main differences among the Afro-Guyanese are those of color, with the mixed group traditionally occupying a slightly higher position in society.

AMERINDIANS The Amerindian group is not uniform, but is made up of people from a number of smaller linguistic and cultural groups. Three indigenous languages are represented among Guyana's Amerindians—Carib, Arawak, and Warrau.

A family of Arawak natives resting in their traditional hut.

Among the Carib-speaking groups found in modern Guyana are the Akawáio, Patamuno (a subtribe of the Akawáio), Arekuna, Parukoto, and Taulipáng (both subgroups of the Arekuna), Ingarikó, and Makushí. The Akawáio live near the Guyana-Venezuela-Brazil border. About 25 percent continue to practice traditional ways, whereas the rest have been converted to Christianity. The Patamuno live in the Pakaraima Mountains between the Ireng River and the Kaieteur escarpment. They have mostly integrated into the Guyanese cash economy.

The Arekuna arrived in Guyana in the 1920s when Seventh-Day Adventist missionaries were expelled from Venezuela. They followed the missionaries and still live in the Paruima area of Guyana. The Parukoto live on both sides of the border with Venezuela and experienced population growth in the 20th century due to missionary work and the introduction of Western medicine. The Taulipáng live near Roraima. This group was almost decimated by the mass immigration of Brazilians into their territory in the mid-19th century. They are still aware of their tribal heritage, but more and more of them speak Portuguese and Spanish as their first languages. The Makushí live in the savannah region of Rupununi and in the southern Pakaraimas of Guyana and Venezuela. They are a large group who have adapted to Guyanese values and technology. The majority practice animism, although some have adopted Christianity. In Rupununi, many are cattle ranchers. The two Arawak-speaking groups are the Locono and Taruma. The Locono live along the coast from the Moruka River in Guyana to the Brazil—French Guiana border. Their population is growing, and they have integrated into the coastal economy of the region.

The story of the Taruma is tragic. They migrated into the southern part of Guyana in the 18th century and were about 500 strong in the 19th century. In the 1920s an epidemic of influenza almost wiped out the Taruma. Today there are a few descendants of this group who still refer to themselves as Taruma. Unfortunately such stories are common because indigenous people with no natural immunity to many European diseases fell sick when Europeans arrived. These diseases were introduced to the Amazon by miners and explorers and spread very rapidly. It is thus remarkable that Guyana's population of indigenous people rose by 22,097 between 1991 and 2002. This represents an annual growth of 3.5 percent. The third group are the Warrau, who live in the lowland delta of the Orinoco River in Venezuela. Unlike forest dwellers, these people are mostly dependent on fishing and are proficient boatbuilders.

An elderly Arawak native and her son have integrated into the new coastal societies of Guyana.

PORTUGUESE Most of the Portuguese indentured laborers came from a single island off the coast of Portugal—Madeira. This is one of the islands of the Azores group. Due to poverty and a tradition of immigration, Madeira has supplied many labor needs around the world from the 19th century to the present.

CHINESE Chinese workers were largely drawn from the south of China and therefore they spoke Cantonese rather than the northern and dominant Chinese language, Mandarin. Much like Madeira, the region of Canton, which is now called Guangdong, has traditionally been poorer than the north and was a major exporter of workers to many parts of the world throughout the 19th and early 20th centuries.

POPULATION PATTERNS

Guyana has an unusual demographic pattern. On the one hand, because 90 percent of the people live in a small area along the coast, Guyana appears to be overpopulated and experiences the problems that accompany that condition—urban crime and inadequate public services. On the other hand, given the actual size of the country, the population density is only about 8.5 people per square mile (3.5 people per square km). That means Guyana is underpopulated and experiences problems associated with having too few people, such as a failure to fully exploit its natural resources because of the lack of labor.

Growth-wise Guyana experienced a fairly constant growth pattern throughout most of the 20th century. The population reached a peak of more than 1 million in the late 1980s. A significant factor in this growth was the introduction of DDT in the 1940s to combat malaria.

ETHNIC TENSIONS

The main ethnic tension exists between the two largest groups, the Indo-Guyanese and Afro-Guyanese. The Afro-Guyanese are generally considered by others—and consider themselves—almost native to the country, whereas the Indo-Guyanese are usually grouped with the Portuguese and the Chinese as "immigrants." These two groups have competed since independence for dominance in politics, with the PPP representing people of East Indian descent and the PNC being largely supported by the Afro-Guyanese.

This ethnic tension is unfortunate but perhaps not surprising given the history of relations between the two groups under colonialism. The British used ethnic and racial differences to prevent groups of workers from uniting against the exploitative planter class. Under extreme economic pressure, ethnic tensions can escalate. If the new government can continue to lead the country out of trouble, there will be another chance for the main groups to work together for a common future.

SOME FAMOUS GUYANESE

REVEREND JOHN SMITH The Reverend John Smith was a member of the London Missionary Society who came to work in Guyana in the early 19th

In 1763 one of the most successful slave rebellions of the century took place in Berbice colony, then under Dutch control. The rebellion started in February that year on the Magdalenenburg plantation and quickly spread to other plantations in the area. By the end of March almost the whole colony was under slave control, and their leaders swore that they would never return to a life of servility and cruelty. One of these slave leaders was Cuffy. Cuffy and the other slaves managed to hold the colony for 10 months despite Dutch efforts to reclaim it. With the help of Amerindians and soldiers from the Netherlands, the colony was finally retaken by the end of the year, and the rebel leaders were rounded up and executed. Cuffy is regarded as a hero in Guyana for his part in this rebellion, and there is a statue of him in Georgetown.

century. He campaigned against the atrocities committed by the planters against their slaves. After a slave uprising in Demerara colony in 1823, he was falsely accused of having helped the slaves to rebel. He was imprisoned and died in prison. His death added fuel to the abolitionist movement—the movement to end slavery—in Britain.

WALTER RODNEY On June 23, 1980, Walter Rodney was given a people's funeral in Guyana. He was a historian who graduated from the University of the West Indies and later received his doctorate from the University of London. He wrote about the history of European exploitation and imperialism in the Caribbean and in his own country. He was also a founding member of the WPA, and this earned him the animosity of the dictatorial government of Forbes Burnham.

Government forces were widely believed to have been involved in his assassination. Despite a government directive that no civil servants should attend his funeral, thousands of people accompanied his body on the day of the funeral. He joins other great Afro-Caribbean writers who have analyzed the role of Europe in creating poverty in the Americas. He became a symbol of the oppression of the Burnham government.

LIFESTYLE

Vendors selling various types of personal goods at the central marketplace in Georgetown.

WITH SUCH A DIVERSE ETHNIC MIX, it is impossible to generalize about the Guyanese people and their lifestyle. The most important differences are those between rural and urban dwellers and between Indo- and Afro-Guyanese cultures. Some social institutions are shared by all the Guyanese, such as education and health, but even in these areas, there are some differences.

FAMILY STRUCTURE

There are three main patterns of family life in Guyana, and they correspond roughly to ethnic and class groupings. Due to different conditions of life under the colonial system, the Afro-, Indo-, and Euro-Guyanese developed different types of family structures or modified those that they brought with them from their country of origin.

AFRO-GUYANESE As slaves, Africans were not encouraged or allowed to maintain their original kinship and family ties, and much of the African culture they came with died out quickly on the plantations. In its place European models were introduced. The Afro-Guyanese are part of what became known as Creole culture, the result of copying European models with modifications due to poverty and economic conditions.

Today Afro-Guyanese family structure has two facets—the reality and the ideal. In the ideal family, young people marry at a formal wedding and then set up house together where the man works and his wife stays at home. The reality for the majority of Creoles or Afro-Guyanese is radically different, however. Because men have not been able to guarantee financial support for their girlfriends, many women have chosen not to marry and instead raise their children (often by several different men) in the homes where the women were born, with their mothers, grandmothers, and sisters to help. Women become the main support of the family, and the men move in and out of this unit, depending on whether they are able to provide some support. This matrifocal, or mother-centered, pattern is common across the Caribbean.

INDO-GUYANESE Both the ideal and reality are also quite different among the Guyanese of East Indian descent. As indentured laborers, East Indians were encouraged to maintain their culture and not mix with either the former slaves or other indentured groups. At the end of their contract, they were encouraged to stay in the colony with grants of small plots of land

A secretary in an office in Georgetown. More and more women are entering the labor force to add to the family income.

near the sugarcane estates. This kept them available for paid work on the plantations and avoided payment of their passage home—which was part of the indenture contract. As more and more East Indians settled in the rural areas, they brought their wives over and tried to re-create their traditional family structure. They managed to keep some of their traditions alive, but some were not sustainable because there were too few of their people.

One cultural trait that was not maintained was the caste system. This is a social hierarchy in which people are considered more or less religiously pure, according to the traditional job held by members of the family. All families doing the same work were considered part of the same caste. In India people generally do not marry outside of their caste, and the rules are very strict, especially in rural areas. In Guyana, East Indians could not continue this custom because there were not enough people from each caste to provide a suitable range of marriageable partners. Nevertheless other features of Indian social life were maintained, including religion and a strong family life. Today the Indo-Guyanese place a great deal of emphasis on marriage, children, and maintaining ties with the extended family. Marriages are no longer arranged by the parents. Young people assert their right to choose their own partners. However, both sets of parents do get involved in preparing for the wedding and helping the young couple get started in life.

Since the Indo-Guyanese can be either Muslim or Hindu, they used to marry only within their religion. That is still the ideal and the norm, but marriages across religious lines are possible, if not encouraged. What is not allowed by families is marriage into other ethnic groups, particularly Creole society. In this way culture has been preserved from one generation to the next. Hindu weddings are common colorful events on the weekends in rural areas during the dry season.

EURO-GUYANESE The third cultural pattern is the one set by European immigrants. In Guyana, as in other colonies, the Europeans were the wealthiest and could afford elaborate weddings and stable marriages. Their ideal was to marry only people of high rank and white ethnic background. Family ties are important because this group is so small today that they must rely on one another for help.

HINDU MARRIAGES IN GUYANA

After the prospective bride and groom have convinced their parents to accept their choice of partner, the young people step aside and the older generation takes over. There are many steps that have to be followed for the wedding to conform to the rules of the Hindu religion and the local traditions of the family or village. Some of the events that make up a wedding in Guyana include:

Chekai (che-KAI) or engagement ceremony: The bride's father offers gifts to the groom's father and a religious scholar known as a pandit invokes the blessings of Hindu gods and goddesses. Other male members of the community are present to show that they approve of the marriage.

Tilak (TEE-lahk): Another ceremony that takes place at the groom's house. The pandit will ask the groom to behave himself and dedicate his life to his bride.

Hardi (HAHR-dee): The bride and groom are purified by pandits, and neighbors bring small gifts to each house.

Kumari-patra (koo-MAHR-ee PAH-trah) and kumar-patra (koo-MAHR PAH-trah): These ceremonies are held to mark the end of childhood for both bride and groom.

Baryat (bar-YAHT): This is the arrival of the groom at the house of the bride. He wears a Western suit with a traditional covering, called a jama (JAH-mah), and a special headdress called pat mauri (PAT MOW-ree).

Milap (MEE-lahp): The baryat is received 15 to 20 yards (14 to 18 m) from the bride's house. The bride's father pays the groom's father a sum of money.

Janwas (JAHN-wahs): Formal welcome of the groom's party.

Dwar pooja *(DWAR POO-jah): A ceremony performed at the door of the bride's house that welcomes the groom and asks for the blessings of all the gods.*

Parchay *(PAHR-chee): The bride's mother welcomes the groom inside the house.*

Naichu *(NAI-choo): A gift-giving ceremony when everyone present offers gifts to the bride seated under the nuptial pole. She is usually dressed in a beautiful traditional Indian dress called a sari, a long piece of fine fabric wrapped around her waist and thrown over one shoulder. She also wears a* choli *(CHOH-lee) or small, tight-fitting, short-sleeved T-shirt and lots of gold jewelry.*

Vivah *(VEE-vah): The older brother of the groom promises to take care of the bride and she is told to respect him as her older brother.*

Kanya dan *(KAHN-yah DAHN): This ceremony is to "give the maiden away." It takes place under the* marua *(mah-ROO-ah). The bride sits beside her father and he places her hand into the hand of the groom, who accepts it. Then the bride moves to sit beside her new husband.*

Lava havan *(LAH-vah HAH-vahn): Lava (fried rice) is burned in the* havan, *or fire pit, under the nuptial pole. The bride and groom throw rice into the fire while the pandit recites sacred texts.*

Bhanwar *(BAHN-wahr): The bride and groom walk around the pole seven times, with the bride in the lead for four circuits and the groom leading for three. This creates a sacred tie between them, with Agni, the fire god, as witness.*

Sat bachan *(SAHT BAH-chahn): The groom makes a vow to look after the bride and consult her in all important family matters. Then he puts* sendoor *(SEN-door), a special paste, on the part in her hair and gives her a ring. This completes the ceremony.*

Sometimes, at this point, the bride leaves to change into a formal white Western wedding dress and goes away with the groom to begin their married life. Not only does a Hindu wedding involve many steps and rituals, but it is also highly religious, with a pandit presiding over nearly every phase. It involves members of both families and the wider community. Marriage is thus far more than just two young people getting together.

Mati-kore (MAH-tee KOR-ay) or "Digging the Dirt": This is performed a couple of nights before the wedding at both the bride's and groom's houses. The women of the family, including the mothers of the bride and groom and their aunts, meet at each other's houses to sing Hindi songs and play traditional instruments. On the way home, they pick up dirt and carry it into their houses. Both groups of women also plant a green bamboo pole, called a nuptial pole, in each of their courtyards. The bamboo signifies the continuity of the family. In the bride's house, the marua, *or the booth where the wedding will be performed, is built on this night and a pandit lights a sacred fire there.*

RURAL VERSUS URBAN LIVING

Most of the Indo-Guyanese live in small rural villages along the coast. Here traditional rites and festivities are maintained more strictly and family ties are broadened with each generation's marriages. A marriage here means not just the union of two young people, but also of their families. This is the basis for social cohesion.

In urban centers marriage is still important and still involves the two families, but may not be as significant in terms of economic cooperation and the inheritance of land and other forms of wealth. Creole people live in both cities and villages, but are more urban than rural. In general urban families are smaller due to the constraints of housing. At the same time there are more families that include the father, since men are more likely to find work and be able to live near both their families and their jobs.

Rural families are often poorer, but live in better conditions than the poor of the cities, who must contend with unsanitary conditions and higher crime rates. Crime is more prevalent in the cities because people can hide in crowds and because the concentration of people attracts those who wish to live by illegal means. In the countryside, because people know one another, it is not so easy to get away with crimes against your neighbors. The benefits of city living include easier access to education and other services and greater potential for paid employment for those who do not have land in the countryside.

The interior (*above*) and exterior (*opposite*) of an Amerindian home located near the Berbice River.

HOUSING

Housing styles reflect wealth and local conditions. Traditional building patterns on the coast have left a heritage of beautiful, raised wooden houses in cities such as Georgetown. Farther inland, houses take on different shapes, depending on their location, from the more ranch-like designs in the savannah to conical, thatched Amerindian houses in the more isolated settlements. The rural poor may not have electricity and will rely on kerosene, gas, and oil lamps for lighting. For cooking, they use kerosene, wood, and coal.

Formal dress for men in Guyana used to require a long-sleeved cuffed shirt and trousers. In the intense heat and humidity of the tropics, this was not a comfortable option. Since independence political leaders have been popularizing a type of shirt called a shirt-jac. This is buttoned up but not tucked in and has at least three pockets on the front. It is white or some other light color and made of light fabrics such as cotton. The pockets can be decorated with pleats, but otherwise the shirt is unadorned. It is also open in a "V" at the top, with lapels. As a more practical formal dress, the shirt-jac has become quite popular with Guyanese men.

Students assembled in a room at an Ursuline convent and orphanage in Georgetown. Besides the national schools, missionary groups also contribute to the education of young Guyanese.

EDUCATION AND LITERACY

Guyanese children are given free education from the age of 3 years, 6 months, to early adulthood. The government spends about 8.5 percent of its GDP (2006) on education, believing that education raises the standard of living for the people. Elementary education covers the first six years, while secondary education begins at 12 years of age and lasts for five to seven years, divided into two cycles of five and two years. Enrollment figures in 2006 were 110,500 in 422 elementary schools, and 70,800 in secondary, technical, and teacher-training education. Guyana boasts a very high literacy rate of 98.8 percent for people over the age of 15.

The school system had suffered from severe underfunding, as well as staffing and supply problems after Burnham made them public in 1976. During the economic crisis of the 1980s, however, the quality of education declined tremendously. Student scores plummeted in the 1990s. There are several reasons for this deterioration.

The main problem is that the government did not have the money to fund a completely free system. School buildings were not properly maintained, and

AN ALTERNATIVE LIFESTYLE: PORK-KNOCKERS

Pork-knockers are a rare breed of men who spend their lives in Guyana's interior, sifting through river mud looking for rough diamonds and gold nuggets. Pork-knockers used to be mostly Afro-Guyanese, but in recent years, with the failing economy, young Indo-Guyanese are trying their hand, too. The gold-miners use pumps to dredge the silt from the bottom of the river into pans with mesh at the bottom. The silt is then separated from larger pebbles and rocks, some of which contain gold. The miners then melt the gold nuggets together and, when they have enough, make their way into the nearest settlement to sell their hard-earned riches.

Diamond hunters dig holes along the riverbanks and sort through the mud and rocks looking for gems. Although Guyana's diamonds are small in size, they are of high quality. The largest diamond ever found, in 1970, was eight carats, but it mysteriously disappeared. The three men who found that diamond are still pork-knockers and are as poor as ever. Although the pork-knockers are constantly finding gold and diamonds, they never get rich, because when they sell their treasures, they spend all their money immediately, eating, drinking, and living well after spending weeks in the jungle. This is much the same pattern as what happened during the gold rush in the United States in the 19th century. It's a different way of life and definitely not for everyone!

there were shortages of textbooks and teaching materials. Under the PNC dictatorship, schools were also used to promote party politics and loyalty. Teachers who did not agree were fired, leaving fewer qualified teachers and an atmosphere of insecurity in the teaching profession. Since the ERP was implemented to repair the economy, Guyana lost many of its professionals, including teachers, to immigration. All of these factors helped create a poor learning environment. The situation has improved somewhat thanks to external funding and an increased education budget from the government in the 2000s.

Students in Guyana undergo a four- to seven-year program to prepare for the basic Caribbean Examination Council (CXC) examination or the London General Certificate of Education (GCE), Advanced Level. Beyond secondary school there are several technical and vocational institutes and two

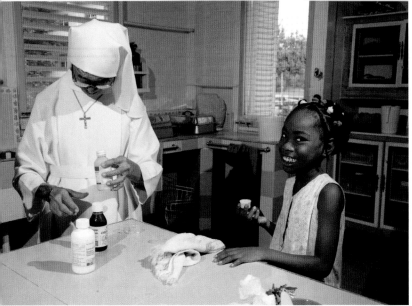

teacher-training colleges, as well as a national university. The University of Guyana was set up after independence. It is free to Guyanese citizens and offers undergraduate degrees in the arts and sciences and a master's degree in history.

HEALTH

A recent Guyana-Cuba scholarship program promises to provide more than 300 medical doctors, nurses, technicians, and pharmacists for Guyana's medical services by 2011.

A nun administers vitamins and other medication to a young girl. The current government aims to improve the overall health-care system in Guyana. However, hospitals and clinics can be hard to find in the rural areas, so much is left to the teachers and caregivers of each village.

The health sector now receives 10 percent of total government expenditures to maintain high-quality health care. Some of its key partners are Pan American Health Organizer (PAHO), the World Health Organization (WHO), the United States Agency for International Development (USAID), and the Centers for Disease Control (CDC).

Guyana is a tropical country that is vulnerable to many of the most infectious and deadly diseases known to humankind. Dengue fever is on the rise and typhoid is also dominant all around Guyana. Gastroenteritis, a disease of the stomach and intestines, is common, as are intestinal parasites. One intestinal parasite prevalent in Guyana is microfilaria, which, if it is not treated, causes noninfectious elephantiasis, the extreme growth of parts of the body to the point where they cannot be structurally supported. Malaria is no longer a problem along the coast, but it is still very common in inland areas above 2,953 feet (900 m). Malaria is passed on by the anopheles mosquito when it bites humans. Certain kinds of malaria are fatal. Yellow fever is also present, and many types of skin fungal infections are endemic due to the high humidity and lack of medical treatment. Tuberculosis has plagued Guyana for a long time, and the government has sponsored several antituberculosis campaigns. This disease is highly contagious and difficult to control. There are also occasional hepatitis epidemics in populated areas.

There is a small group of people who believe in the powers of a specific ritual to cure sick people, particularly those with emotional and psychological problems. The ritual is called Kali Mai Puja. Puja is an East Indian word for a religious ritual that shows devotion to one of the Hindu gods or goddesses. In this particular ritual, people pray to the goddess Kali for help. Kali is believed to be the goddess of destruction, but she can also destroy evil. A Kali Mai Puja requires a specialist called a pujari *(POO-jah-ree) to preside over the activities.*

This person can be of either gender and can come from any cultural background. Followers of Kali Mai say that the rituals are drawn from all the religions in Guyana and therefore can work for anyone. Kali Mai works through possession by spirits and animal sacrifice. There is even a Kali Mai Church, and the only requirement for membership is for a person to reject his or her former religious beliefs. Some psychologists have used Kali Mai pujaris *to help with their patients' problems. Although not widely popular, this is a distinctly Guyanese religion and an alternative healing practice.*

Many of these diseases, especially in coastal areas, result from inadequate supplies of water and inadequate public hygiene. Most rainwater and used water is collected in open drains in the cities and towns. In richer neighborhoods sewage is disposed of through septic tanks, but in the poorer areas, it is allowed to run off in open drains. Similarly, garbage is allowed to pile up in public places in poorer areas. Stagnant water and garbage encourage the spread of diseases such as typhoid, dengue, gastroenteritis, and parasitic infections. Public water supplies are also unsafe in both rural and urban areas.

Some Guyanese turn to an alternative healing practice called *Kali Mai Puja* (KAH-lee MAI POO-jah). Kali Mai, also known as Mother Kali, is a goddess of South Asian origin that is presently worshiped in numerous churches. Healing rituals and services are an integral part of Kali worship which attracts many devotees because of their desire to alleviate any number of problems. Worship of Kali occurs every Sunday at various churches or *mandirs* where a *puja* is performed for all the deities housed in the *mandir*, and is then followed by a number of different healing services.

RELIGION

A cathedral in Georgetown.

A S WITH ETHNICITY, DIVERSITY is the key to religion in Guyana. Almost all of the world's main religions have some representation in the nation, along with minor cults and folk belief systems. Religion has played an important role in historical and modern-day political relations among the various groups.

Sunday service at Saint Andrew's Presbyterian Church in Georgetown.

THE MAIN FORMAL RELIGIONS

Current statistics show that 57 percent of Guyanese are Christian, and most of them are Pentecostals (17 percent, 2002 estimate). Hindus represent 28.8 percent of the population and are mainly of East Indian descent. Muslims make up 7.3 percent, and although most are East Indian, there are a few Afro-Guyanese Muslims as well.

CHRISTIANS The Anglican Church is the official church of England, and the religion was brought to Guyana by British planters during the colonial period. Anglicanism was the state religion of British Guiana until independence in 1966. The Anglican Church is similar to the Roman Catholic Church in many ways, but Anglicans do not regard the Pope as the head of the church. The English monarch (currently Queen Elizabeth II) has the constitutional title of Supreme Governor of the Church of England. Most Creoles adopted this religion while they were slaves and continue to practice it today. Since all education in Guyana was controlled by church groups until 1956, there was some pressure for East Indian children to convert while they attended school. Some did so, but most have held on to Hinduism and Islam, their religions of birth.

Catholic Guyanese children saying grace before their meal.

HINDUS Hinduism is the dominant religion in India. It is a pantheistic religion, which means that there are many different deities, or gods. There are three major sects in Hinduism: Saivism, Vaishnavism, and Shaktism. Lord Siva is regarded as the chief deity in Saivism. Followers can be identified with a mark of three horizontal stripes across their foreheads. The East Indian immigrants to Guyana belonged to the Hindu sect of Vaishnavism. Adherents of this sect regard Lord Vishnu as the supreme creator. They can be identified with a U-shaped mark and a long stripe between the two arms of the U across their foreheads. Followers of Shaktism worship Devi or the Mother Goddess as the creator of all. Since 1875 there have been two schools of Hinduism— Sanatan Dharam or the Orthodox school, and Arya Samaj or the Reformist school. Followers of Sanatan Dharam believe in the most traditional of Hindu writings and practices. They worship all the traditional gods and goddesses, such as Ganesha, Lakshmi, and Agni, and believe that at the top of the hierarchy of gods are Brahma (the Creator), Vishnu (the Preserver), and Shiva (the Destroyer). Hindus believe that the human spirit is reincarnated many times, meaning that it is born into many bodies and lives many lives. Each time the soul comes to Earth, it becomes more and more religiously pure.

Eventually the soul becomes as pure as the gods themselves and enters *Saccidandanada* (sach-ee-ahn-AHN-dah), a state of perfect spiritual

Saint George's Anglican Cathedral in Georgetown dates from 1889.

Children of Indian ethnicity come together to worship their Lord Shiva during a Hindu celebration.

existence that requires no further incarnations. As the soul travels through its incarnations, it is classified according to its religious purity into one of four groups called *varnas* (VAHR-nahs)—Brahmin (BRAH-min), Kshatriya (SHAH-tree-ah), Vaishya (VAISH-yah), or Sudra (SOO-drah). These *varnas* are ranked, with Brahmin at the top. Within each *varna* are a number of subdivisions called castes. Although the caste system was not maintained among immigrants to Guyana, East Indians continue to recognize those born in the Brahmin group as the only legitimate religious leaders for their community. As the purest souls, only Brahmins can be pandits or priests of the Hindu religion.

Arya Samaj or Reform Hinduism was started in India in 1875 by Swami Dayanand Saraswati. The main differences between the two schools are that the reformists reject many of the practices of the Orthodox religion as superficial. For example, Arya Samaj Hinduism preaches that the three major gods—Brahma, Vishnu, and Shiva—are different facets of one god and that the minor gods are not gods at all, only humans who reached a high state of religious purity. For Reformists, worship involves meditation and yoga, rather than making offerings to idols or statues of the gods. The Reformists do not believe that a person is born into a *varna*. Rather they argue that a person becomes a member of one of the *varnas* as a result of his or her actions on Earth, so that a very virtuous person can become Brahmin.

MUSLIMS A minority of the Indo-Guyanese are followers of Islam. Islam is a religion that was started by Prophet Muhammad in Arabia in the seventh century A.D. Islam has spread around the world, especially to the east, from its origins in the Middle East. Muslims believe in one God, Allah. Their holy book, written in Arabic, is called the Koran. Muslim men attend prayer meetings in mosques.

Women do not enter mosques, although they must pray regularly. The Muslim holy day is Friday, and Muslim holy men are called imams. Although Hindus and Muslims in India have had a long history of ethnic strife and have even fought a civil war, relations between the groups in Guyana are amicable.

OBEAH Some Afro-Guyanese practice a folk religion called *obeah* (oh-bay-ah) based on African beliefs. Believers practice magic and believe that obeah priests have special powers drawn from traditional African gods and spirits. Obeah is based partly on the African concept that the ancestors have spirits that can affect the lives of the living and that relations between these two worlds have to be kept in good order. Practitioners wear charms or spells to protect themselves from harm. Obeah was made legal in 1970.

A Muslim Guyanese walking into a mosque for evening prayer in Georgetown.

INDIGENOUS BELIEFS Among Amerindians there are a number of indigenous beliefs. Amerindians have faced intense pressure from missionaries to convert to Christianity as part of the "civilizing" process. Sometimes this pressure has had disastrous consequences, as in the case of the millennial movement started by Awacaipu, a shaman of the Arekuna tribe. Shamans play a significant role as healers and advisors to their villages. They are sought out to detect sorcery and combat evil. Some groups have remained more isolated and have managed to maintain their belief systems. They have pantheistic religions. The gods are usually represented by natural phenomena, such as waterfalls and animals such as the jaguar. Amerindian religion stresses a respectful relationship between humans and the gods, who are evident in natural forms.

Throughout the 19th century, European churches sent many missionaries to the Americas to try to convert indigenous people to Christianity. Often their influence was direct, in the form of missions established in the interior of countries such as Guyana. However, their teachings were sometimes indirectly powerful, as individuals carried their ideas back from trading posts or settlements. One such incident took place when Awacaipu, a shaman of the Arekuna tribe, returned from living in Georgetown. He had been employed by Sir Robert Schomburgk (1804—65), a German scientist and traveller with the Royal Geographical Society. Awacaipu had learned English and was very impressed by the teachings of the European missionaries.

When he returned to his group, he told them of the coming of the millennium, which Amerindian shamans believed was a new age of material plenty. In Awacaipu's version, the millennium would bring the power of white people to Amerindians. However, those who would enjoy this advantage must first die within a stipulated three-day period, to resurrect with new white bodies to meet their families at the slopes of Mount Roraima. They would rule over other brown-skinned men who had not undergone this ordeal. A few hundred followers clubbed one another to death over the next three days. When the dead people failed to reappear after two weeks, the survivors turned on Awacaipu and killed him. Millennial movements such as this have been common wherever colonialism reached indigenous people whose lifestyle was radically different from that of the Europeans. The result was often that the indigenous people believed that Europeans possessed magic and only through extreme practices such as suicide could they become like the Europeans.

CULT GROUPS

Cults are religious groups that indoctrinate their members into total loyalty and obedience to their leaders. They can be very dangerous to society if their intentions are not honorable. Two such groups have unfortunately made Guyana their home in recent history.

Under the Burnham dictatorship, Guyana was home to two cults, both started by Americans. The more famous of these to the outside world was the People's Temple of Christ, led by Reverend Jim Jones. Jones brought

As with Awacaipu, other Amerindians traveled to missions and learned about other religions. One of these, a Makushí from the savannah region, brought back stories at the end of the 19th century of a god named Papa (as in "Father") who lived in the sky. He had a vision in which Papa told him to start a new religion called Hallelujah and spread it. Other groups picked up parts of the religion from the Makushí. One ritual, the thanksgiving ceremony, is still being practiced in the interior.

When hunters return with a good catch, they gather the animals and fish inside a hut that has been cleansed with water. Then they form a column outside the hut and begin to chant and drum to Papa, singing and dancing to songs and prayers taught by the Hallelujah prophets. When they have nearly reached the hut, they form a line, each man with his hand on his neighbor's shoulder, kneel, and pray to thank Papa for giving them a successful hunt. This is clearly a combination of native and Christian elements. Ironically, when missionaries reached the interior, they failed to recognize this ceremony as partly Christian and tried to ban it.

the People's Temple to Guyana in 1974 with plans to set up an agricultural commune in the northwest of the country. Since this was territory disputed and possibly threatened by the Venezuelans, and because Jones claimed to be a friend of Jimmy Carter, who would soon become president of the United States, Burnham allowed the People's Temple to buy land and establish its commune. The cult came to the attention of the media in 1978 when an American congressman, Leo Ryan, died under mysterious circumstances while investigating the cult in Guyana. That day, November 18, 1978, Jones convinced or compelled 914 of his followers to take cyanide in a mass suicide. Even children were found poisoned, and some members of the cult were found murdered.

The second cult group is less known outside Guyana, but has had devastating effects on politics within the country. It was called the House of Israel and was started by "Rabbi" Edward Washington, an African American wanted by the Federal Bureau of Investigation (FBI) for a number of crimes, who fled the United States in 1972. His real name was David Hill, and he convinced Burnham that he was a political refugee escaping a racist campaign

Many of the followers of the People's Temple of Christ were African Americans, and Jones committed the full support of the cult to Burnham's dictatorship. Relations between the cult and the Guyanese government were dubious, as the cult was allowed to import drugs and weapons with no interference from the authorities.

against him. The cult was based on the belief that blacks were the original Jews and had the right to occupy Israel. Cult followers were indoctrinated to believe in the supremacy of blacks over other groups and to prepare for the day when other groups would be killed. There were about 8,000 members, and they were protected from the law by their close ties to the PNC. Cult members wore uniforms that showed the colors of the PNC—black, red, and green. They were used by the government to disrupt legal strikes and to harass people perceived to be in opposition to the dictatorship.

On July 14, 1979, a cult member named Bilal Ato killed an English Jesuit priest and photographer for the *Catholic Standard* newspaper, Father Bernard Drake, in full view of spectators. Burnham refused to investigate the murder and took three years to bring Ato to court, where he was defended by a state prosecutor and received a lighter sentence than his actions demanded. Walter Rodney was one of the few who openly denounced the crime and accused the government of being behind it. The cult continued to function as long as Burnham lived. After his death the government of his successor tried to soften the dictatorship and arrested cult leaders for crimes committed years earlier.

Under the cover of religion and dictatorship, these cults were given the right to operate in Guyana despite their illegal activities. The Guyanese people do not want a repeat of this situation in the future.

CHURCH AND STATE

Under the 1980 constitution, all Guyanese enjoy freedom of religion. There is no official state religion. Nevertheless the major religious organizations have tended to associate themselves with political parties and have become quite involved in the daily political life in the country. There are both Hindu and Islamic religious associations that have openly sided with both major parties, the PNC and the PPP, although the Indo-Guyanese have traditionally supported the PPP. The most vocal critics of the PNC dictatorship were the Christian churches and their umbrella organization, the Guyana Council of Churches (GCC). Today, with less political tension, church groups have been able to relax their pressure on the government.

FOLK BELIEFS

Besides formal religions, there are a number of folk traditions in Guyana. One in particular has captured the imagination of all ethnic groups. Stories about Anansi, a spider god from the Ashanti culture in West Africa, delight children of all backgrounds. Anansi, or Nancy as he is known in Guyana, is popular throughout the Caribbean. He is a trickster god, who is neither good nor evil. In the stories, he gets himself in trouble and uses his quick intelligence to escape. One of his archenemies is the tiger. Some people have linked these stories to slave life, arguing that Nancy represents the slave, who is weak and must use cunning to survive, and the tiger represents the master, who is strong.

LANGUAGE

A young local woman on a public phone with a mobile phone in her hand.

CHAPTER 9

MANY DIFFERENT LANGUAGES are spoken in Guyana today, including some examples of a type of language called Creole. Many of these languages did not originate in Guyana, but over the years, they have come to reflect Guyana's unique human environment. In this chapter, we will consider how and why such a small country has so many different ways of communicating, and also learn about different forms of communication such as proverbs and the media.

English-language signboards are found all over Guyana.

Geographically Guyana is part of the South American continent, but culturally and historically it has more in common with English-speaking Caribbean islands such as Trinidad and Tobago. In fact it is often classified with the Caribbean countries as part of the geographical region known as the Caribbean Basin. The reasons for this confusion in regional identity are many. To begin with the Guianas (French, Dutch, and British) were the only non-Spanish and non-Portuguese colonies on the South American mainland. They are small and are dwarfed by their much larger Spanish- and Portuguese-speaking neighbors, Venezuela and Brazil. When people think of South America, they rarely remember that not all of it is actually part of Latin America.

Guyana's colonial heritage and modern linguistic and cultural makeup make the nation "feel" more Caribbean than anything else, and this sense of identity is perhaps more important than the technicalities of geographical regions. In this way language outweighs geography in giving the Guyanese their identity in the modern world.

DIFFERENT LANGUAGES

English is the official language of Guyana, making the country an anomaly on the predominantly Spanish-speaking South American continent. As well as formal English, many other languages are spoken in Guyanese homes and in the streets. The majority of Guyanese people also speak a version of English known as Creole, Creole English, or Guyanese. Creole is a language that develops when people who speak different languages live near one another and need to communicate. In Guyana, Creole English contains many influences from the other people and cultures that have contributed to Guyanese life and history.

English is the most widely used and official language in Guyana.

Areas such as the Caribbean Basin and the Guianas were ideal for the development of Creole languages because so many people speaking so many different languages and dialects were brought together to work on plantations. Although the dominant linguistic influence was that of the master class, workers of African, Asian, and other descents were able to influence the language they used among themselves on the estates. For this reason, there are French, English, and Dutch Creoles in the Guianas.

Because Creoles are young languages, they often have relatively simple vocabularies. As a result many people mistakenly assume that they are not true languages and undervalue their cultural significance. In fact Creoles are just as rich as other traditional languages, and people who speak them can express as much of a range of meaning and subtlety as any person speaking a traditional language. Increasingly Creoles are becoming the language of postcolonial literature and thought in countries where they are prevalent.

For example, Dutch words that are still used today include *koker* (KOH-ker), which means "water gate," and *stelling* (STEL-ling), a "wharf" or "quay." Not surprisingly these words describe things that were originally introduced and built by the Dutch. Although the French occupied Guyana for only a short time around the turn of the 18th century, they left a linguistic heritage in the word for "rowboat," *bateau* (BAH-toh). Portuguese migrants have also left their linguistic mark in everyday language. Apart from some words for foods, there are also words such as *briga* (BREE-gah), used to describe someone who wants to fight, and *olhado* (ohl-YAH-doh), which means "evil eye." Chinese immigrants have mainly influenced the language with terms for food. There are dozens of Amerindian words in use, particularly as place names, since these people were the first to settle the territory. Other Amerindian words include *warishi* (wahr-EE-shee), which refers to a basketwork backpack, and *benab* (BEN-ahb), meaning "hut." From the languages of the Indian people who made the voyage to Guyana, words such as *typee* (TY-pee), meaning "a strong love," and *carahi* (kah-rah-HEE), meaning "a type of stewing pan," have entered everyday speech.

Many Guyanese use Creole English to communicate on the streets.

Some words from African languages have also come down through the generations, including *te-te* (teh-teh), a type of skin disease, and *kerreh* (KEH-reh), a state of power. Some common expressions in Creole English include *aw right*, which means "hello" and "okay;" *me no know* means "I don't know;" and *just now* means anything from "right away" to some time much later.

Although English is the official language and Creole English is the language spoken by most people on the streets, other languages are still spoken in the home and within certain ethnic communities. A second Creole language found only in Berbice is a Dutch Creole left behind after many years of Dutch colonial occupation of the country. Sometimes just called "Berbice," this language is nearing extinction as its speakers die. It is a combination of Dutch, a Nigerian language, and Amerindian. Another dying Dutch Creole is found in the Essequibo region and is known as Skepi. About half the words are similar to the words found in Berbice, but speakers claim that the two languages can't be mutually understood.

In many Indo-Guyanese homes, you can still hear one of the two main Indian languages that were spoken by the original immigrants—Hindi, Urdu, and Caribbean Hindustani (a dialect of Hindi). These are the languages spoken by the majority of the people. The Amerindian minority also speaks a number of languages and dialects based on the three main language/culture groupings found there—Arawak, Carib, and Warrau. Some specific Amerindian languages and dialects include Akawáio, Kalihna, Makushí, Patamona, Pemon, Waiwai, and Wapishana.

VOICE OF THE PEOPLE: THE *CATHOLIC STANDARD*

Under the dictatorship of Forbes Burnham, all significant print media were controlled by the PNC or the PPP, with the notable exception being the Catholic Standard. *This meant that there was only one public voice that tried to report the news accurately with no party bias. The paper was edited by Catholic priests, many of whom risked their lives to report and publish the news.*

Many of these priests, particularly those acting as editors, faced death threats and some, such as Michael James, an assistant editor in 1979, were assaulted. Father Bernard Drake was killed while serving as a photographer for the paper in 1979. These men performed an invaluable public service, bravely bringing the news to Guyana and financing the paper with international donations. The Catholic Standard *is still published, but under much improved democratic conditions. It has a circulation of about 10,000.*

THE MEDIA

For many years the media in Guyana were directly owned by the government. Guyana Television Broadcasting Corporation provides limited service and supplements the two satellite relay stations that bring American television to Guyanese audiences. The Guyana Broadcasting Corporation (GBC)—the single radio station—is also owned by the government. There was once another station, Radio Demerara, but the government bought it in 1975. In 2004 the GBC and Guyana Television (GTV) merged to form a new company, National Broadcasting Company Limited (NCN Inc.). There are about 420,000 radios in the country, and radio broadcasts are an important source of news and information for many people.

In the print media, the government owns the only publishing house, Guyana National Printers Ltd. It also owns the only daily newspaper, *Guyana Chronicle*, which it bought in 1974. There are other news weeklies and periodicals. The most significant of these are the *Mirror*, published by the PPP; the *Catholic Standard*, published by the Catholic Church; and the *Stabroek News*. The *Mirror* was, for many years, the voice of the official opposition to the dictatorship, as it represented the views of the PPP, while the *Chronicle* directly reflected the views of the PNC government. The *Catholic Standard* was, until 1986, the only paper not linked to a political party. Under Burnham's rule, both these papers were harassed through accusations of libel and through limitations on the amount of newsprint they could purchase. Since newsprint is imported, the government could prevent it from being delivered to rival papers. Even donated newsprint was often denied to these newspapers.

In 1986, under Hoyte, the *Stabroek News*, began operations and was printed overseas in Trinidad. The money for newsprint and other operating costs was raised in other countries—the first donation was made by the National Endowment for Democracy, an American foundation. It was printed weekly and shipped to Guyana. This marked a new beginning for relations between the press and the government.

There are about 205,000 Internet users in Guyana (according to a 2008 estimate). This figure is likely to increase as service providers compete for subscribers.

A young Guyanese woman using the Internet to keep up with the books she reads.

NAMES TELL A STORY

Guyana and its cities have been called by many different names throughout their long history. The basis for the name Guyana came from the Amerindian name for the whole region—Guiana. This word means "land of many waters," an accurate description of this area, as there are close to 7,000 square miles (18,130 square km) of inland water besides 285 miles (459 km) of the Atlantic Ocean fronting its coast.

Georgetown has also gone by different names. Although it was founded by the English, the French were the first to name it, calling the settlement "Longchamps." When the Dutch took it back from their French allies, they named it "Stabroek," and the old town market is still known by this name. When the English took back Guyana for good, they renamed their colonial capital "Georgetown" after a British monarch. Inhabitants have also called their city "Mudtown," which describes what used to happen to the streets after the seasonal rains. A map of Guyana shows the influences of various cultures. There are names left over from the Dutch and English, such as New Amsterdam and Queenstown, and others that have come from Amerindians, such as Roraima and Kaieteur.

FOLK WISDOM AND PROVERBS

One heritage that is particularly African is the use of proverbs in regular speech. Because they were not allowed to have a formal education or write, slaves used oral tradition to pass on their cultural values. This is still evident today in the many proverbs that people use to communicate with one another. Proverbs are short metaphors that capture an essential idea about right and wrong or a story about how the world works.

Young children enjoying a good folktale.

An example of an Afro-Guyanese proverb, written in Creole English, is "Two hill doan meet but two men does meet," meaning that people can come together, unlike immovable hills. Another example: If a parent accuses a child of doing something wrong and the child confesses to another infraction out of guilt, the parents will say, "Empty gun ah shoot guilty man," meaning that their false accusation actually caught the child because he was guilty.

ARTS

A painting by Guyanese artist Bernadette Persaud.

GUYANA IS A SMALL COUNTRY and has never been a rich one. This has limited the extent to which the government has been able to sponsor artistic activity. Nevertheless there is a vibrant popular culture, complete with music and dance traditions from different ethnic groups and time periods. Literature has also thrived within the Caribbean tradition. Amerindians also contribute to the visual arts and crafts to make up a kaleidoscope of artistic possibilities.

Woven handicrafts made by the Arawak tribe.

In Guyanese housing design, the kitchen was always built in the back of the house in a separate, concrete-reinforced room. This was because wood stoves were the most common way to cook and presented a fire hazard in wooden homes. The demands of safety and a hot climate created typical Guyanese houses, which today are still an attractive feature of older sections of Georgetown.

VISUAL ARTS

Probably the oldest art in Guyana, the Timehri rock paintings are one of the nation's most valuable Amerindian legacies. Located on a quartz cliff face near Imbaimadai (on the Karowrieng River, a tributary of the Mazaruni in western Guyana), the rock paintings (petroglyphs) are a collection of roughly painted animals, symbols, and handprints that are believed to date back to A.D. 1300.

Petroglyphs in Rupununi Savannah.

Some of the animals portrayed include sloths, accurately depicted hanging upside down from a vine, and anteaters. There are also abstract symbols such as squares, zigzags, and strings of lozenges (diamond shapes). At the base of the cliff there are hundreds of handprints in red paint. There are so many of these that they overlap. Although these are clearly the work of prehistoric Amerindians, modern Amerindians in the area have a different story to explain Timehri. They say that the paintings were done by their supreme god, Ama-livaca, who visited the area during a great flood. The paintings extend over an area that is 50 feet (15 m) wide and 25 feet (7.6 m) high and are so impressive that the name of this cliff was chosen for Guyana's international airport when it was renamed after independence.

Aubrey Williams, one of Guyana's best-known modern painters, also draws inspiration from the Amerindian past and present. He claims to have Amerindian blood and came to know the Warrau people quite well when he served as an agricultural officer in their district. He spent two years with the Warrau and was even initiated into their tribe. His paintings reflect his knowledge of Guyana's interior, with its steamy primeval forests and

powerful rivers. Other Guyanese painters include Donald Locke and Denis
Williams, who moved to Europe to paint and write.

ARCHITECTURE

Guyana's older cities and towns are notable for their distinctive architecture.
The oldest and most valued buildings are all made of wood. The coast
was originally forested, so there was an abundant supply of this material.
However, pine was often imported for construction because it reacted to the
tropical climate better than some of the locally available hardwoods. Pine
was also easier to work with when carpenters did not have power tools and
it was light enough to not sink into the alluvial mud of the coast.

Guyanese houses combined European styles and the demands of the local
environment. Because stone or concrete structures would have sunk into the
mud, even large public buildings had to be made of wood. Some incredible
feats of engineering were accomplished in Georgetown. Saint George's
Cathedral, for example, is the tallest wooden church in the world. Its spire
reaches 132 feet (40 m) into the air.

HOUSING DESIGN IN GUYANA

As various generations of Guyanese adapted to living on the hot, humid, and flood-prone coast, a number of architectural innovations helped make life cooler, drier, and safer. The first innovation in colonial housing was to copy local Amerindian designs and build the house on stilts. This kept the home out of the mud and away from flood waters. The area beneath the house could be used for animals or storage. Until very recently, houses were all made of wood. They were oriented to take advantage of the winds blowing from the northeast off the ocean. There were also special windows and shutters called Demerara windows. These are shutters that are hinged at the top and built out from the wall of the house. Between the shutter and the wall are moldings with decorative cut-out designs and a small tray at the base.

The holes in the moldings allowed for the passage of air, while the tray was used by wealthier houseowners for blocks of ice so that when the breeze blew over the ice, it would become cooler and thus cool the room inside. Ice was brought from North America and was stored in sawdust or sand until needed. The front of the house was dominated by a covered verandah that had shutters and jalousies to allow air to circulate. A jalousie is a system of louvers that can be set at different angles. In this way, the whole wall was open to the sea breezes.

This may not seem very high when one considers the concrete and steel skyscrapers of today, but to try to build something so high without a system of reinforcement (such as steel beams) or a deep basement is not easy. Guyana's colonial architects and carpenters managed to overcome this difficulty. Although much of their work has been destroyed by termites and fire over the years, there are still some impressive examples of this distinctly Guyanese art and craftsmanship.

A 19th-century house in Georgetown.

MUSIC

Music is perhaps Guyana's richest cultural treasure. All the different groups have contributed their musical sense and instruments to Guyana's national musical repertoire. For example, Portuguese immigrants brought both their *rajaos* (rah-JOWZ; a type of banjo) and *braggas* (BRAH-gahs; small guitars) with them to the new land. One type of music that has been credited to them is *santapee* (SAHN-tah-pee) music.

Probably the most common element in Guyanese music is the drum. Amerindian religious ceremonies, such as the hallelujah rite, depend on the drum to set the rhythm and keep the beat. The Afro-Guyanese still use the drum extensively in a variety of musical forms. One of the better-known types of music to come out of Guyana and other Caribbean countries is that of the steel band, which relies exclusively on percussion instruments or drums to make sound.

The Guyana Music Festival was held biannually from 1957 to 1979. Neglected for close to 30 years, there were several attempts to revive it in recent years. In October 2007 Guyana successfully launched the Guyana Music Festival. Local people as well as Caribbean artists gathered to perform various music styles such as soca, calypso, shanto, and reggae. Vocal solos, duets, verse speaking, choral speaking, school and church choirs, folk songs, steel pan players, and gospel groups all came together to make the festival an unforgettable experience.

The Indo-Guyanese have also brought their traditional music and instruments, including the sitar, a stringed instrument that must be placed on the floor to be played because it is so long. Traditional Indian music is often played to accompany dancing.

DANCE

As with music, Guyana enjoys traditional dance forms from many lands. The *kathak* (KAH-tahk) is a traditional East Indian dance form that is performed by women. It is a highly stylized form of classical dance and requires years of training. The dancers are accompanied by traditional music.

Two distinctly African dances that made the crossing of the Atlantic and are still performed today are the *que-que* (kwe-kwe) and the *cumfa* (KUM-fah). The *que-que* is performed by groups at weddings and other public celebrations. The group splits into two, with each side asking and answering questions about the people involved in the event. This can be quite humorous for the participants and spectators. *Cumfa* is a quasi-religious dance accompanied by drumming. The participants dance in a rhythmic fashion until they begin to fall into a trance. They believe that drums can summon supernatural forces and spirits that enter the bodies of the dancers. *Cumfa* is not performed as a public dance but in private among those who believe in the power of the drums and the dance.

CRAFTS

The Amerindian heritage and contribution is notable in Guyanese crafts. Indigenously produced crafts include basketry, floor mats, and chairs made of woven reeds and grasses. Amerindian hammocks from the interior are also highly prized.

These remarkable creations are extremely light weight and can expand to incredible widths because of the natural fibers used and the technique of weaving. The sleeper can also use the extra material as a blanket so that the hammock becomes a complete bed. However, because hammocks take a long time to make, most Amerindian weavers prefer to keep them for personal use.

An Amerindian weaver weaving a basket.

Other writers who are from Guyana but are not part of the tradition of anticolonialism include Wilson Harris, who has published two books based on the oral traditions of the Carib and Arawak Amerindians (*The Sleepers of Roraima*, 1970, and *The Age of the Rainmakers*, 1971) and a novel about travels to the interior during the colonial period in Guyana (*Palace of the Peacock*, 1960).

Other crafts produced in Guyana include brassware and gold filigree. Brass objects are made using a technique of beating or pounding the metal into shape. This takes not only skill but great strength and stamina, and results in beautiful bowls and trays. Gold is also worked into filigree jewelry. Filigree work is a technique where gold is rolled into fine wires, which are then shaped into intricate designs and patterns. The work is painstaking and must be done by hand.

Some of Guyana's valuable woods are also used in furniture production. Both the green and purple heartwood trees make sturdy and beautiful pieces. The most highly prized wood is *wamara* (wah-MAH-rah), a type of brown ebony that is very hard and durable.

LITERATURE

The most significant trend in 20th-century literature in the Caribbean and Guyana has been *negritude* (nay-gree-TOOD). This is a French word coined by Aimé Césaire, a black intellectual from the Caribbean island of Martinique. Césaire, along with other thinkers from Africa and Léon-Gontran Damas from Guyana, were students in Paris in the 1930s. This talented group was especially interested in the work of other black artists and writers and started a trend toward awareness of ethnicity and history in the arts. Negritude was a poetic term that was meant to stress the significance and beauty of black art from both Africa and the New World.

One of the writers who most inspired this group and their successors in the negritude tradition was René Maran of Guyana. Maran's novel *Batouala* (published in 1921) was openly anticolonialist and written from the black viewpoint. It caused quite a scandal in literary circles but also won the Prix Goncourt, a renowned French literary prize. In response to the anticolonial debate surrounding Maran's work, the students formed an anticolonialist magazine called *Légitime Défense* (*Legitimate Defense*) that was published from 1932 to 1934 in Paris. From then on, negritude and black pride were significant forces in the literature of the Caribbean. The most recent addition to the historical tradition of negritude was Guyana's Walter Rodney. His academic and journalistic contributions to Guyana were cut short. He was killed by a bomb in his car while running for office in the elections of 1980.

JANET ROSENBERG

Janet Rosenberg (1920—2009) was a Jewish girl who married an Indo-Guyanese named Dr. Cheddi Jagan. She came to British Guiana in December 1943 and became involved in the labor struggle, working with labor hero Hubert Nathaniel Critchlow. She became Guyana's first woman president in 1997 but resigned after 20 months due to ill health. She authored several publications on the history of the PPP. There are five children's storybooks to her credit, including When Grandpa Cheddi Was a Boy, Children's Stories of Guyana's Freedom Struggles, *and* Alligator Ferry Service. *Jagan received the Mahatma Gandhi Gold Medal in recognition of her struggle for peace, democracy, and women's rights from UNESCO in 1997.*

Not all of Guyana's modern writers were influenced by Parisian culture. Edgar Mittelholzer sought the roots of his colonial identity in London, which he visited in the 1940s. His most famous work is *Morning at the Office*, published in 1950. Other writers, such as Denis Williams, found their inspiration and cultural roots in Africa. Williams is famous for his book *Other Leopards* (1963). Karen King-Aribisala is remembered for winning two Commonwealth Book Awards (Africa Region) for *Our Wife and Other Stories* (1991) and *The Hangman's Game* (2008), which is based on the heroic revolt by African slaves against their British colonial masters in 1823.

LEISURE

During their spare time, the locals enjoy shopping at Stabroek indoor market in Georgetown.

>>> THE GUYANESE HAVE AN interesting and unique approach to life that aims to balance work and leisure. Although most people are not wealthy, they still have many options for entertainment in the home and community. Family plays an important role in many leisure activities. The Guyanese also participate in sports and have inherited one of their most popular games, cricket, from the British.

Children enjoying a swim in Lake Capoey.

HINDU THANKSGIVING AS A SOCIAL EVENT

At certain times in life, people want to give thanks for the happiness and good fortune they have experienced. Hindus do not have a single thanksgiving day to do this. They can hold small family thanksgivings called jhags *(JAG) whenever there is a reason. For example, when a child is born and later has his or her first haircut,* jhags *are held by families who can afford them to celebrate and give thanks.*

A jhag *is nominally religious in nature, since a pandit is hired to read from the holy books and talk about religious matters. However,* jhags *are also social occasions when members of the extended family gather to socialize and celebrate successes in the family.* Jhags *can last up to five days and are accompanied by singing and feasting. A* jhag *is a social as well as a religious event and is a part of making life.*

MAKING LIFE

In the Guyanese language, a distinction is made between "making a living" and "making life." These two expressions refer to the two aspects of life that the Guyanese consider essential. The first, "making a living," has the same meaning as it does in standard English and refers to working in order to provide food and other essentials for oneself and one's family. The second phrase, "making life," refers to socializing and taking care of other members of the family and the wider community. Making life can mean anything from chatting with a neighbor to lending a hand when needed or participating in village or community events.

Both aspects of life, the economic and the social, are highly valued and the Guyanese strive to maintain a balance between them. It is considered unhealthy to focus more on making a living and to ignore making life. People who are perceived to do this are considered to be greedy and antisocial. Likewise people who only make life without working to make a living are called "limers" or are said to be "liming." This means that they are living off their friends and relatives and are not pulling their economic weight. There are a number of ways of making life in Guyana.

One of the most popular pastimes available to all Guyanese is going to the local store or marketplace to chat with neighbors. Older men with time on their hands, especially, gather at popular spots in town to talk with each other. No other activity is necessary to make this a satisfying leisure activity. Younger men can often be found at bars, called "rum houses," where they meet to share a drink and play dominoes. Although women are not traditionally part of these male groups, they too meet to share the day's news, often at the market where they may be engaged in selling produce.

There are some ethnic differences in how people entertain themselves. For Afro-Guyanese youth, one of the most popular ways to spend a weekend evening is to go to a dance. Many villages have community centers where dances are held regularly, and towns often have mobile discos (movable sound systems) that can be hired for any event. Among East Indians, the tradition of public dances is not so popular because young women are not supposed to go out without a chaperone. However, people of all ages enjoy going to the cinema to catch the latest Indian movie. There is also a religious-based social event called a *jhag*.

In Georgetown there are several more recreational options. The Botanical Gardens and the seawall are popular for taking a stroll in the cool evening. Both of these public parks have bandstands where the Police Force and Defense Force bands sometimes play for the public. In addition, there are cinemas, museums, and theaters. Swimming in the ocean along the most populated stretches of the coast, however, is not popular because of the pollution from the drainage ditches and the silt from rivers and seawalls.

Guyanese men playing dominoes at the market square in Georgetown.

The Song of Guyana's Children

Born in the land of the mighty Roraima,
Land of great rivers and far stretching sea;
So like the mountain, the sea, and the river
Great, wide, and deep in our lives would we be;

Onward, upward, may we ever go
Day by day in strength and beauty grow,
Till at length we each of us may show,
What Guyana's sons and daughters can be.

Born in the land of Kaieteur's shining splendor
Land of the palm tree, the croton, and fern,
We would possess all the virtues and graces,
We all the glory of goodness would learn.

Born in the land where men sought El Dorado,
Land of the Diamond and bright shining Gold,
We would build up by our faith, love, and labor,
God's golden city which never grows old.

Thus to the land which to us God has given
May our young lives bring a gift rich and rare,
Thus, as we grow, may the worth of Guyana
Shine with a glory beyond all compare.

ANANSI AND HATE-TO-BE-CONTRADICTED

Hate-to-Be-Contradicted was very bad-tempered, and every time someone came to visit him, he would tell them ridiculous lies about his palm nut tree so that they would contradict him. When they did, he would hit his visitors with sticks because he hated to be contradicted. When Anansi came to visit, Hate-to-Be-Contradicted played the same game with him, but this time the story had a different ending. Anansi agreed with Hate-to-Be-Contradicted and told him a big lie about his okra trees. Hate-to-Be-Contradicted was going to contradict Anansi, but since he himself hated to be contradicted, he just agreed and said he would like to visit Anansi to see if the lie was true.

He arrived at Anansi's house and found all of Anansi's children telling big lies about where their father was. This made Hate-to-Be-Contradicted very angry, but finally Anansi came back. They fed Hate-to-Be-Contradicted a stew with so many peppers that he cried out for water. One of the children went to get water but came back without any. The child said that he could not get water, because in the water jug, the water at the top belonged to his father, the water in the middle belonged to his aunt, and the water at the bottom belonged to his mother. The child said that if he did not take the right water, it would be sure to cause a fight. Hate-to-Be-Contradicted got very angry with this ridiculous story and told the child he was lying. When Anansi heard this accusation, he ordered his wife and children to beat Hate-to-Be-Contradicted, because although he hated to be contradicted, he had just contradicted someone else and therefore deserved to be beaten. They beat him until he shattered into little pieces, which scattered across the land. That is why today there are many people who hate to be contradicted.

Children gather after school to play various games together. They especially enjoy activities such as kite-flying and simple games that they make up. They also play some of the sports that are popular in Guyana, such as cricket, field hockey, basketball, and soccer. Guyanese people of all ages enjoy singing and music as part of their social activities. There is a large repertoire of popular songs and music, and even songs just for children or for parties. Storytelling is a traditional pastime that is dying out as more people turn to radio and television for home entertainment.

Young boys playing soccer on a lawn in Georgetown.

SPORTS

By far the most popular sport in Guyana is cricket. This game originated in England hundreds of years ago and spread to most British colonies. The Caribbean colonies did not take part in the sport internationally until the 1920s, when the West Indian team was recognized as an international class, on the side of Britain. Guyana is one of the countries that has always contributed players to the West Indian team. Famous Guyanese cricketers include Roy Fredericks and Clive Lloyd. In recent times, the main heroes have been locals Carl Hooper and Shivnarine Chanderpaul, who hail from the Bourda Georgetown Cricket Club. Founded in Guyana in 1858 it is also the longest-surviving cricket club in the entire Caribbean. Soccer and baseball are also popular in Guyana. Another sport played with a ball and stick is field hockey. Field hockey sticks are rather different from ice hockey sticks and a ball is used instead of a puck. Field hockey is often played by girls as well as boys. Other sports that enjoy some local club support are basketball, rugby (similar to American football), tennis, swimming, and karate.

Horse racing is a popular spectator sport. Races in Britain are broadcast in Guyana and people love to bet on the horses. The local newspapers devote as much space to the races as they do to national politics. The Guyanese also like two other types of races—motor racing and goat racing. The Guyana Motor Racing Club holds international motorcycle and car races every March and October. Much less glamorous is goat racing, which is a local sport not found elsewhere.

A sport that attracts mainly foreigners is sport fishing. Although tourism is only now being promoted officially, the government has already acted to protect the environment and is discouraging the export of rare and endangered animal species.

CRICKET, ANYONE?

Cricket is a ball-and-bat game that is popular in England and in former British colonies where children learned to play the game in colonial schools. The rules of the game are rather complicated and can be difficult for nonplayers to understand. Basically the game is played by two teams of 11 players each. They play on an oval field called a pitch with two wickets, one at either end of the pitch. A wicket is a set of three posts or stumps in the ground on which are balanced two bails, or shorter sticks. Each team tries to keep its bails balanced on the stumps throughout the game. A bowler throws the ball and a batsman uses a paddle-shaped bat to try to hit the ball into the field. Unlike in baseball, the batsman holds the bat quite low to defend the wicket that he stands in front of. If he hits the ball, he can score "runs," which are worth points in the game.

The batsman can be "dismissed" (similar to being "out" in baseball) from the game if the bowler hits the wicket with the ball, if a fielder catches the batted ball before it hits the ground (like catching a pop fly in baseball), if the batsman breaks the wicket with his own body or uses his body (instead of the bat) to defend the wicket, or if a member of the other team breaks the wicket while the batsman is attempting a "run."

Games are called matches, and they can last for days, since each inning is very long. An inning—there are only one or two in a match—ends when the 10th batsman is out, when a certain number of balls has been bowled, or when the batting team captain volunteers to end the inning. Players use padding to protect their legs from errant balls.

FESTIVALS

A traditional Indian dancer at a Hindu festival in Georgetown.

BESIDES HOLIDAYS SUCH AS New Year's Day, Christmas, and Good Friday, the Guyanese also celebrate days that are important in their country's history. Hinduism and Islam also contribute official holidays to the list. Recognizing minority beliefs in this way serves to unite the Guyanese people in celebration.

The choir of Saint Andrew's Presbyterian Church sing their hymns to the beats of the steelpan (steel drum).

CHRISTIAN FESTIVALS

The two most important celebrations in the Christian world are Christmas and Easter. Both are related to the life of Jesus Christ. Christmas marks the birth of Jesus and is celebrated on December 25 with family feasting and gift-giving. Easter, including Good Friday and Easter Monday, is a time to reflect on how Christ died for people's sins. Friday is the day he was crucified and Sunday is when he was resurrected. Although these are Christian holidays, everyone in Guyana takes part in the festivities.

Christmas is one of the biggest celebrations in the country. There are more festivities in the countryside than in the towns because people in rural areas have more time and know their neighbors well. Bands in costume called masquerade bands also travel through the towns. The music is accompanied by limbo dancers. Limbo dancing is a Caribbean favorite that involves trying to bend over backward to dance below poles held at various heights by other people. The best limbo dancers are true acrobats, since the objective is to avoid falling down or touching the pole. The music is produced by flutes and drums. People also visit each other's homes and wish one another Merry Christmas and Happy New Year.

Girls decorating a Christmas tree to bring festive cheer during the season.

Easter has become a time to enjoy activities such as kite-flying and country fairs. In Georgetown it has become popular to go to the seawall to watch musical groups perform. Because Easter is celebrated as a four-day weekend, people enjoy the extra time they get to spend with families and friends.

HINDU FESTIVALS

Holi Phagwah is the celebration of the new year and beginning of spring in India. It is similar in some ways to April Fool's Day because the festivities include trying to make people feel foolish by covering them with red- and yellow-colored powder and spraying them with colored or plain water. Kama, the Hindu god of love, is the deity celebrated at this time, which also makes the holiday similar to Valentine's Day. For children it is a fun time since they can spray people with colored water and powder in the streets.

Divali (Dewali, Deepavali), also known as the Festival of Lights, is celebrated by Hindus around the world. It is a celebration in honor of Lakshmi,

A band parades on the road, playing music during a Holi Phagwah celebration in Georgetown. Holi Phagwah is a Hindu-Caribbean celebration of the new year to mark the beginning of spring.

Hindu girls in their beautiful costumes during Divali.

the goddess of wealth and prosperity. At this time Lakshmi is said to return home from her summer residence in the mountains and lights are lit to help her find her way. Another reason for the lights is the story of an Indian king, Lord Rama, who was banished from his kingdom for 14 years. At the end of his banishment, he returned to reclaim his land, but it was the darkest night of the year, so the people lit up the night. Divali celebrates his return. This holiday may be celebrated on different dates, but it always falls in the month of October or November.

MUSLIM FESTIVALS

Islam follows a lunar calendar. This calendar is not synchronized with the standard solar calendar, so important religious dates are not linked to the months of the solar year. This means that over time, these dates move, so they cannot be tied to regular seasons. The Islamic calendar marks a number of important days based on the life of the Prophet Muhammad—who revealed the teachings of the religion to the people—and other significant dates in religious history.

Religious practice in Islam is based on the "Five Pillars of Faith." These rules determine daily religious practice and inspire the major celebrations of

Muslims believe that the prophets of Judaism and Christianity are also prophets of Allah. They respect these prophets and the stories of their lives. One such man was Abraham, who was asked by Allah to sacrifice his son (called Isaac in the Bible story) to prove his faith. He was ready to do this, but at the last moment, Allah told him to stop and provided a ram to be killed instead. Muslims believe Ishmael is an ancestor of Muhammad, so this story is very important to them. To celebrate the day of sacrifice Muslims prepare meat to eat with their families and to give to the poor to represent both the sacrifice of Abraham and to fulfill the Third Pillar of Faith. This is also called the Great Feast (the Lesser Feast is Id al-Fitr, which ends Ramadan).

the religion. The First Pillar of Faith is that there is only one true god, Allah, and Muslims must affirm this in their daily practice. This revelation was given to Muhammad on the "night of power," about 10 days before the end of the month of Ramadan. This is celebrated in Muslim homes as Laylat al-Qadr. The Second Pillar of Faith is that Muslims must worship Allah five times a day.

The Third Pillar of Faith is that every Muslim must distribute charity to the poor. Although this can be done at any time of the year, there is a special celebration for it called the Feast of Sacrifice, or Id al-Adha. This is one of the officially recognized Islamic holidays in Guyana. The Fourth Pillar of Faith is that all Muslims should fast during the month of Ramadan. This is the month when the Koran, or the Muslim holy book, was revealed to Prophet Muhammad. To show respect, Muslims do not eat or drink during the daylight hours. The family comes together to eat in the evenings. Id al-Fitr, or the Feast of Fast-breaking, marks the end of Ramadan. This is the most joyous family celebration in the Islamic calendar, when everyone comes together to feast and celebrate the end of the fast. The Fifth Pillar of Faith is the hajj, or religious pilgrimage to Mecca, a holy city in Saudi Arabia. Every Muslim must try to make the trip once in his or her life.

Although not related directly to the Pillars of Faith, Muslims also celebrate the day of Muhammad's birth, called *Yum an-Nabi*. This is also an official holiday in Guyana, although it is celebrated only within the Muslim

This celebration is also known as Ashura or Hosay in other parts of the Muslim world. It is a 10-day series of events that marks the death of Hussein, one of Muhammad's sons. The culmination of Ashura is a procession that reenacts the burial of Hussein, complete with a replica of his domed tomb. Muslims carry the tomb around town, and if they are close to water, they may set it afloat. Tadja was once quite important in Guyana's villages, but this celebration often coincided with Hindu celebrations. When this happened, people often ended up in fights, as each group tried to push the other out of the way. The colonial government banned Tadja in 1930.

Since independence, Tadja has been practiced peacefully, with other groups participating, but it is now in danger of dying out even among Muslims as the younger generations move away from the countryside and the traditional practices of their parents and grandparents. In other parts of the Caribbean, such as Jamaica and Trinidad and Tobago, Tadja is called Hosay and has become a celebration of East Indian—both Hindu and Muslim—unity.

community. There are special recitations about the life of Muhammad in the mosques and feasting among family members. A Muslim festival that is now dying out in Guyana, but one that was once the cause of interethnic strife in the countryside, is the Tadja.

HISTORIC HOLIDAYS

There are four major historic holidays in Guyana. The first holiday of the year is February 23, which celebrates the founding of the republic on that day in 1970. This was when independent Guyana adopted a new constitution and declared itself a republic within the Commonwealth of Nations. Of all the historic holidays, this is the most festive. It is marked by such festivities as calypso contests, costume competitions, and picnics. Calypso is a type of Caribbean music where the words are quite important to the music. The highlight of the day is a parade of floats. Companies sponsor the building of

A CALENDAR OF OFFICIAL HOLIDAYS

New Year's Day	January 1
Anniversary of the Republic	February 23
Holi Phagwah	February/March
Good Friday and Easter	March/April
Labor Day	May 1
Independence Day	May 26
Caribbean Day	first Monday in July
Freedom Day	first Monday in August
Divali	October/November
Christmas Day	December 25
Boxing Day	December 26
Id al-Fitr	varies
Id al-Adha	varies
Yum an-Nabi	varies

floats that follow different themes, and these are then brought together for a parade in Georgetown that is judged for best float. Many people participate in the construction and decorating of the floats, and many others come to watch the parade.

The next historic holiday of the year is May 26—Independence Day. This marks the day that Guyana became free of British colonial rule in 1966. Caribbean Day is celebrated in early July and is a time when people reflect on what it means to be part of CARICOM and the Caribbean cultural community. In early August, Freedom Day is celebrated. This commemorates the emancipation of slaves in 1834 and is celebrated by games and African drumming. People also eat African foods on this day to celebrate the African contribution to Guyanese culture.

FOOD

Fresh produce for sale in the markets of Guyana.

>>T HERE ARE AS MANY CUISINES in Guyana as there are cultures. Each group of people has brought something of their homeland and food preferences with them, and many of these "ethnic foods" have entered the standard repertoire of all Guyanese people.

AMERINDIAN TRADITIONS

Most of the Amerindian groups who still practice their traditional culture are horticulturists who clear small areas of land in the jungle to plant crops. Their staple crop is the cassava (manioc), a root crop that is

Cassava and other daily essentials being sold in the market square at Georgetown.

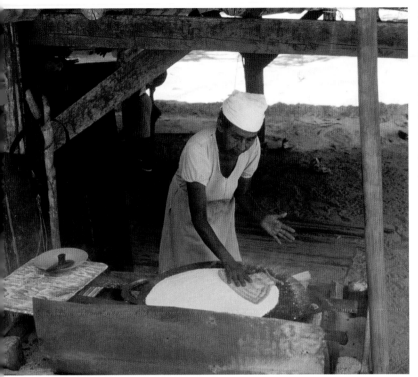

native to the jungle. When cassava is raw, it contains prussic acid, which is poisonous to people. To remove the poison, Amerindian women first rub the root across a board studded with sharp stones. This grates the hard tuber into shreds, which are then squeezed to remove the juice. The leftover pulp can then be ground into flour and used to make bread, which looks like a large pancake.

This bread is cooked on large flat pans over a fire. A flat bread does not contain yeast to make it rise. The poisonous juices are boiled in ceramic pots so that the poison is absorbed by the clay. What remains is one of the ingredients of Guyana's national dish, pepperpot. Pepperpot is a type of stew that also includes meat cooked for days over an open fire with lots of pepper. Cassava can also be used to make a type of alcohol called *casiri* (KAH-see-ree).

An Arawak woman makes cassava bread. Cassava is the staple food for most Amerindian groups, but they also hunt, fish, and gather fruits in the forest to supplement this diet.

COASTAL CUISINE

About 90 percent of the Guyanese live in the settled coastal strip. The many different cuisines in this area are a reflection of the variety of cultures that live there.

EAST INDIAN The East Indians brought their curries and *dahls* (DAHLS) with them, and today many Guyanese consider these standard food in their homes. Favorite meat curries in Guyana are mutton, prawn, and chicken. *Dahls* are stews made with legumes such as lentils. These, like curries, involve the blending of lots of flavors and are cooked for a long time. The staple accompaniment to curry and *dahl* is rice.

A popular festive food is "cook-up," which is any kind of meat prepared in coconut milk and served with rice and beans. Coconut milk requires a lot of labor to prepare and is very rich, so it is not eaten every day in most homes. Another Caribbean food that reflects an East Indian heritage is *roti* (ROH-tee). These are large turnovers made with a flat bread and filled with curried meats and potatoes.

Indian Guyanese tucking into a feast of fragrant jasmine rice, meat, and bean curries on a banana leaf.

CHINESE AND PORTUGUESE Both the Chinese and Portuguese have also contributed to the Guyanese menu. Guyana boasts of some excellent Cantonese restaurants run by its Chinese inhabitants. Noodle dishes are very popular. The Portuguese have contributed a variety of foods, including garlic pork, *bacalhau* (bah-cah-LAU,), *bolo do mel* (BOH-loh doh MAYL), garlic soup with egg, and couscous. *Bacalhau* is salted codfish and can be prepared in stews and soups. *Bolo do mel* is a cake made with molasses, a by-product of sugarcane processing.

Couscous was probably brought to the islands of Madeira from north Africa, where it is a staple food, before making the journey to Guyana. It is made from cracked wheat and can be flavored or plain. Pumpkin is used as both a fruit and vegetable in Guyana, and the Portuguese fry it to make pumpkin fritters. As Catholics, the Portuguese observe Shrove Tuesday (the Tuesday before Good Friday) by eating special pancakes called *malassados* (mah-lah-SAH-dohs) and *sonhos* (SOHN-yohs).

AFRICAN The African heritage is also apparent in the use of yams and okra in many dishes, including *callalu*. *Foo-foo* (foo-foo) comes directly from Africa and is a type of cake made from plantains. *Metagee* (MEH-tah-gee) is another coconut milk—based stew that includes yams, cassava, and plantains.

OTHER FOODS Because Guyana is a coastal country, seafood figures prominently in Guyanese kitchens. The best catches are shrimp, red snapper, and sea trout. All of these can be prepared in a number of ways and served with rice and peas. From the interior comes good quality beef and freshwater fish. Guyana also grows red and green peppers, green onions, eggplant, celery, avocados, tomatoes, and breadfruit.

Women choose their fish from the catch of this fish vendor in New Amsterdam.

DRINKS

As well as distinctive food, Guyana has several local drinks. The local beer, called Banks, has won many international awards. Banks is a brand that originated in Barbados, but is produced locally in Georgetown, too. A sugar-producing country, Guyana makes an excellent rum known as Demerara. An internationally famous cocktail was also concocted in Guyana. Called the Brown Cow, it is nine parts Tia Maria (a sweet coffee liqueur) and one part milk.

Children enjoy local soft drinks such as Banko Shandy, a ginger beer, and Malta Vita, another popular local beverage. Guyana also grows a variety of fruits that make delicious juices, including oranges, grapefruits, pineapples, mangoes, tangerines, and watermelons.

SHOPPING

Every city and town has a central market where most people shop for their food and other household needs. The largest of these is Stabroek Market in Georgetown, which was built by the Dutch. Here sellers and buyers gather every day to haggle and bargain for food and other household supplies. Small producers of fruit and vegetables also ply the streets selling their wares or give them to children to sell after school.

Since many goods are imported into Guyana and therefore are often in short supply, people try to develop good relationships with local shopkeepers. Sometimes shopkeepers refuse to sell goods that are hard to get to people who are not their regular customers or insist that the customer buy something else at a higher price in order to get the scarce product.

The North American routine of driving to the supermarket where everything is priced and in one place has yet to catch on in Guyana. Most people prefer to buy their food fresh and to shop frequently during the week. They enjoy haggling over prices. This system is also more environmentally friendly, since most food is not packaged, and people bring their own shopping baskets rather than use plastic bags.

Stabroek Market in Georgetown. In smaller towns, there are general stores, marketplaces, and traveling vendors.

GUYANA PEPPERPOT

4 servings

1 lb (450 g) stewing beef or brisket, cubed

1 lb (450 g) pork trotters (pig's feet, optional)

½ lb (225 g) pig tail (optional)

½ cup (125 ml) Amerindian seasoning (cassareep)

1 red hot pepper

1 cinnamom stick

2 tablespoons (30 ml) sugar

Salt and sugar to taste

2 stalks basil

1 bunch fresh thyme

1 large onion, chopped

2 garlic cloves, chopped

- Wash and scald pig tails.
- Put trotters in a pot of boiling water and skim off impurities. When trotter is half tender, add the beef and simmer gently for about one hour until meat is tender.
- Adjust the flavor with salt and sugar.
- Serve with bread or rice.

GLAZED PINEAPPLE RICE PUDDING

3 tablespoons (45 ml) cooked white rice

2½ cups (625 ml) milk

1 egg, beaten

Sugar to taste

1 cup (250 ml) pineapple rings

Fresh cherries

- Cook the rice in milk gently until thick and creamy.
- Cool slightly and add the egg and sugar to taste. Pour into a fireproof dish.
- Drain the pineapples and arrange on top of the rice mixture.
- Put the juice into a pan, add sugar and boil for about 5 minutes or until it is reduced to a glazing consistency.
- Pour it over the pineapple slices.
- Decorate with a cherry in the center of each pineapple ring and serve hot.

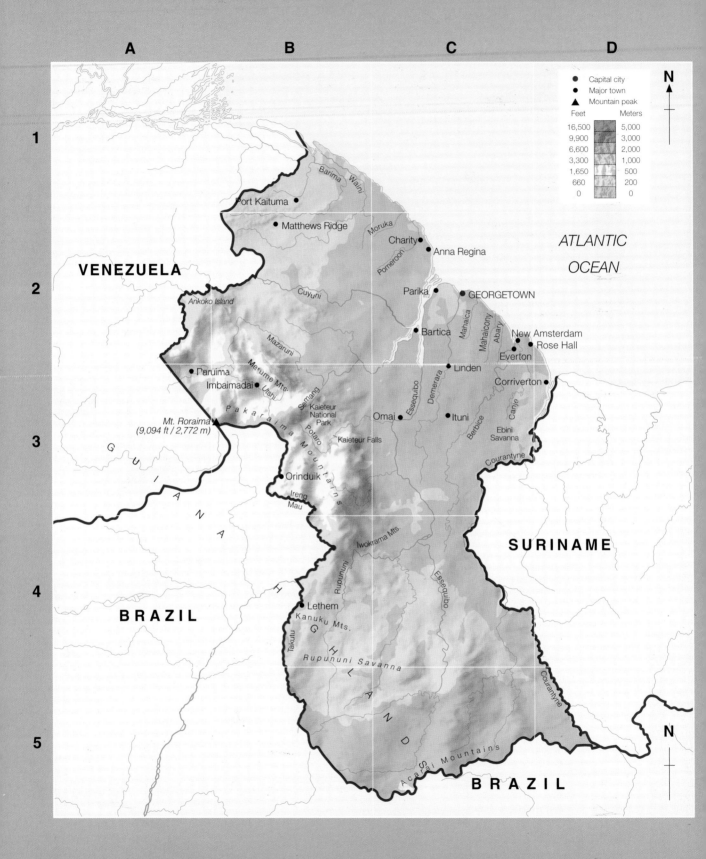

MAP OF GUYANA

Abary RIver, C2
Acarai Mountains, C5
Ankoko Island, A2
Anna Regina, C2
Atlantic Ocean, D1—D2

Barima River, B1
Bartica, C2
Berbice River, C3
Brazil, A4, D5

Canje River, C3
Charity, C2
Corriverton, D3
Courantyne River, C3—C5
Cuyuni River, B2

Demerara River, C3

Ebini Savanna, C3
Essequibo River, C3—C4
Everton, C2

Georgetown, C2
Guiana Highlands, A3—A5

Imbaimadai, B3
Ireng River, B3
Ituni, C3
Iwokrama Mountains, B4, C4

Kaieteur Falls, B3
Kaieteur National Park, B3
Kanuku Mountains, B4

Lethem, B4
Linden, C3

Mahaica River, C2
Mahaicony River, C2
Matthews Ridge, B2
Mau River, B3
Mazaruni River, B2
Merume Mountains, B3
Moruka River, C2

New Amsterdam, C2

Omai, C3
Orinduik, B3

Pakaraima Mountains, B3
Parika, C2

Paruima, A3
Pomeroon River, C2
Port Kaituma, B1
Potaro River, B3

Roraima, Mount, B3
Rose Hall, C2
Rupununi River, B4
Rupununi Savannah, B4, C5

Semang River, B3
Suriname, D4

Takutu River, B4

Utshi River, B3

Venezuela, A2

Waini River, B1

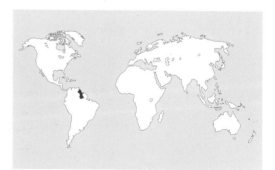

ECONOMIC GUYANA

Services
- ✈ Airports
- 🚢 Ports
- 🧍 Tourism

Manufacturing
- 🥫 Food processing
- 🥩 Meat packing
- 🔩 Metalworking
- 🪵 Sawmill, lumber, and wood products
- 🏭 Sugar milling

Agriculture
- 🐄 Cattle
- 🌴 Coconut
- 🌾 Rice
- 🍬 Sugar

Natural Resources
- 🪨 Bauxite
- 💎 Diamonds
- 🐟 Fishing
- 🟨 Gold

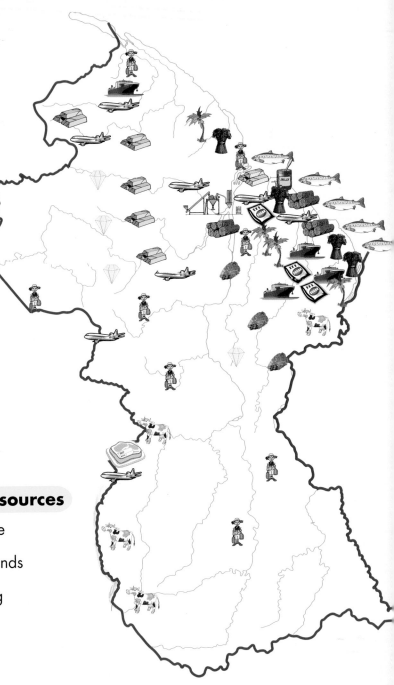

ABOUT THE ECONOMY

OVERVIEW

Guyana is recovering from flood-related contraction through exports of agricultural and mineral products. Foreign investment in the sugar and rice industry and mining sector also aids Guyana's economic recovery. In 2006 Guyana became a member of the CARICOM Single Market and Economy (CSME) to broaden its export market in the raw materials sector. Guyana faces chronic problems such as shortage of skilled labor, deficient infrastructures, and high import costs. As a result export earnings have remained flat and the country is heavily in debt.

GROSS DOMESTIC PRODUCT (GDP)

$2.966 billion (2008 estimate)

GDP GROWTH

3.1 percent (2008 estimate)

LAND USE

Arable land: 2.23 percent
Permanent crops: 0.14 percent
Others: 97.63 percent (2005 estimate)

INFLATION RATE

1.9 percent (June 2009 estimate)

CURRENCY

US$1 = GYD 204.27 (2009 estimate)

NATURAL RESOURCES

Gold, bauxite, diamonds, timber

AGRICULTURAL PRODUCTS

Sugarcane, rice, shrimp, fish, edible oils, beef, pork, and poultry

INDUSTRY

Mining (gold, bauxite, diamonds, timber); agriculture (sugar, rice, livestock, fresh fruits and vegetables); forestry; fisheries; manufacturing (food and beverage, textiles, pharmaceuticals); construction and services (distribution, financial, transportation and communication)

MAJOR EXPORTS

Sugar, gold, bauxite, diamond, rice, fish and shrimp, molasses, rum, and timber

MAJOR IMPORTS

Manufactures, machinery, petroleum, food

MAIN TRADE PARTNERS

Export partners: Canada 18.7 percent; United States 16.5 percent; United Kingdom 9.1 percent; Portugal 7.6 percent; Trinidad and Tobago 5.2 percent; France 4.7 percent; the Netherlands 4.6 percent; Jamaica 4 percent
Import partners: Trinidad and Tobago 26.2 percent; United States 20.5 percent; Cuba 7.2 percent; China 7.1 percent; United Kingdom 5.4 percent

UNEMPLOYMENT RATE

9.7 percent (2008 estimate)

CULTURAL GUYANA

Stabroek Market
The Stabroek Market houses 80,000 square feet (7,432 square meters) of stalls that sell every conceivable item from household goods and gold jewelry to fresh meat and vegetables. Its 19th-century cast-iron clock tower can be seen for miles around and is a famous landmark.

Mount Roraima
Mount Roraima is the highest point in Guyana at 9,094 feet (2,772 m). Located in the Guiana Highlands at the point where the boundaries of Brazil, Venezuela, and Guyana meet, it is the source of many rivers of Guyana, and of the Amazon and Orinoco river systems. The Amerindians call it a mesa because of its giant flat top.

Kaieteur Falls
British geologist C. Barrington Brown discovered Kaieteur Falls on April 29, 1870. Located on the Potaro River within the Kaieteur National Park (established in 1930), Kaieteur Falls is accessible by road, river, or flight. Water initially tumbles 741 feet (226 m) over the edge of a sandstone plateau, then a further drop of 81 feet (25 m) over the great rocks at the bottom, making it the highest single drop waterfall in the world. A rainbow arches eternally over the mist-covered boulders of the gorge. According to Amerindian legend, Kai, a chief of the Patamona tribe, sacrificed himself by canoeing over the falls. It was believed this would encourage the great spirit Makonaima to save the tribe from being destroyed by the savage Caribishi.

Rupununi Savannah
The Kanuku Mountains divide this vast area of dry grasslands, with sparse trees, tall termite mounds, and wooded hills into the North and South Rupununi. Local vaqueros (cowboys) run large cattle ranges that date from the 19th century. Scattered Amerindian villages; a rich wildlife species such as giant otters, black caimans, jaguars; a mind-boggling variety of colorful exotic bird species; and the world's largest water lilies, the *Victoria Amazonica*, are common sights. Exciting water tours by boat are conducted when the rains flood the savannah.

Shell Beach
The beach stretches for 90 miles (140 km) along Guyana's northwestern shore, between the Pomeroon and Waini rivers. Four of the world's eight turtle species, including olive ridleys, hawksbills, and magnificent giant leatherbacks, struggle ashore at night to dig nests between March and July. Each lays as many as 10 dozen eggs among numerous shells before returning to the Atlantic waters. These turtles used to be slaughtered for their meat and eggs but are now part of a nongovernment conservation program.

Cathedral of Saint George
The capital has a spacious and village atmosphere as buildings are mostly two-story wooden houses, all standing separately. The tallest wooden church building in the world is the Anglican Cathedral of Saint George, which was designed by Sir Arthur Bloomfield and consecrated in 1892.

Sea Wall
The flat coastal strip along the Atlantic coast was built up from centuries of sediment accumulation from the large South American rivers. It occupies an area of 6,486 square miles (16,800 square km) and is below sea level by about 6.56 feet (2 m). The low concrete sea wall lines the coast of Guyana to protect Georgetown from the Atlantic Ocean. Colorful advertisements and political jargons cover the walls. On Sundays, crowds gather here to relax, picnic, dance, cycle, or take a stroll.

Iwokrama Forest
The Iwokrama is one of the four last pristine tropical forests in the world. Rain forest flora and wildlife can be observed from the Canopy Walkway, a 505-foot (154-m) network of suspension bridges and decks. The Iwokrama is home to the highest number of fish and bat species in the world. It is also a living laboratory for sustainable tropical forest management.

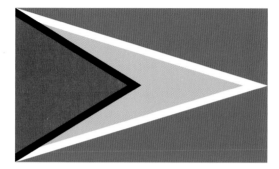

OFFICIAL NAME
Cooperative Republic of Guyana

LAND AREA
17,462 square miles (45,226 sq km)

CAPITAL
Georgetown

POPULATION
779,417 (2009 estimate)

LIFE EXPECTANCY
Total population: 72.56 years
Male: 67.16 years
Female: 78.3 years (2008 estimate)

BIRTHRATE
11.12 births per 1,000 population (2009 estimate)

DEATH RATE
8.31 deaths per 1,000 population (2009 estimate)

AGE DISTRIBUTION
0—14 years: 25.7 percent
15—64 years: 68.7 percent
65 years and over: 5.5 percent

ETHNIC GROUPS
East Indian: 43.5 percent, African: 30.2 percent, Mixed: 16.7 percent, Amerindian: 9.1 percent, Others: 0.5 percent (2002 estimate)

RELIGIOUS GROUPS
Christian: 57 percent, Hindu: 28 percent, Muslim: 10 percent, Other: 5 percent

MAIN LANGUAGES
English, Amerindian dialects (primarily Carib and Arawak), Creole, Carribbean Hindustani (a dialect), Urdu

LITERACY RATE
98.8 percent

IMPORTANT HOLIDAYS
New Year (January 1); Youman Nabi, the Muslim prophet Muhammad's Birthday (early January); Republic Day (February 23); Phagwah, Hindu New Year (March or April); Good Friday/Easter (March or April); Labor Day (May 1); Independence Day (May 26); CARICOM Day (first Monday of July); Emancipation Day (August 1); Divali, Hindu Festival of Lights (November); Christmas Day (December 25); Boxing Day (December 26)

POLITICAL LEADERS
Forbes Burnham: prime minister, 1964—80 and president, 1980—85; Hugh Desmond: prime minister, 1980—85 and president, 1985—92; Cheddi Jagan: prime minister, 1957—64 and president, 1992—97; Janet Jagan: president, 1997—99; Bharrat Jagdeo: president, 1999—present

TIME LINE

IN GUYANA	IN THE WORLD
	1492 Christopher Columbus arrives in America.
A.D. 1498 Christopher Columbus sights Guyana.	**1506** Portuguese control east African coast
	1558–1603 Reign of Elizabeth I of England
1580 Dutch establish trading posts up Essequibo River.	
1620 The Dutch West India Company imports slaves from Africa for its sugarcane plantations.	**1620** Pilgrims sail the *Mayflower* to America.
1780–1813 Guyana changes hands several times among the Dutch, French, and British.	**1776** U.S. Declaration of Independence
	1816 French physician Rene Läennec invents the stethoscope.
1879 Gold is discovered in Guyana.	**1861** The U.S. Civil War begins.
1889–99 Venezuela claims a large portion of Guyana west of the Essequibo River.	**1897** Wilhelm Roentgen, a Bavarian professor of physics, discovers X-rays by accident.
	1914 World War I begins after Germany provokes Europe-wide conflicts.
1950 Dr. Cheddi Jagan founds the Progressive People's Party.	**1939** World War II begins.
1953 Britain suspends Guyana's constitution after the left-wing Indo-Guyanese's Progressive People's Party (PPP) wins parliamentary election.	
1957 PPP splits along racial lines.	**1957** Ghana becomes the first African country to be granted independence.
1961 Guyana granted full autonomy; Cheddi Jagan (PPP) becomes prime minister.	

IN GUYANA	IN THE WORLD
1962 Venezuela revives territorial claims. **1963** Racial violence between people of African origins and Indian supporters of Jagan. **1966** Guyana is granted independence with Burnham as prime minister. **1978** Mass suicide of 900 members of a religious cult led by Jim Jones at Jonestown. **1980** Guyana gets a new constitution, and Burnham is appointed Guyana's first executive president. **1985** Desmond Hoyte (PNC) becomes president following the death of Burnham. **1992** Cheddi Jagan (PPP) is elected president. **1997** President Jagan dies and is replaced by Janet Jagan. **1998** Georgetown in state of emergency after violent racial riots **1999** Bharrat Jagdeo becomes president after Janet Jagan resigns for health reasons. **2006** President Bharrat Jagdeo is reelected for another term. **2007** United Nations tribunal rules that Guyana and Suriname shares a potentially oil-rich offshore basin. **2008** President Jagdeo signs trade agreement with the European Union (EU).	**1966** The Chinese Cultural Revolution **1969** U.S. astronauts land on the moon. **1986** Nuclear power disaster at Chernobyl in Ukraine **1991** Breakup of the Soviet Union **1997** Hong Kong is returned to China. **2001** Terrorists crash planes in New York, Washington, D.C., and Pennsylvania on September 11. **2009** Outbreak of H1N1 flu around the world. World leaders at the UN Climate Change Conference, held at Copenhagen, sign a climate-change treaty.

GLOSSARY

Anansi
A spider trickster god who is popular in African tribal folklore.

arapaima **(ah-rah-PAI-mah)**
A freshwater fish that can grow up to 10 feet (3 m) long and weigh 440 pounds (200 kg).

bragga **(BRAH-gah)**
A small Portuguese guitar.

callaloo **(kah-lah-LOO)**
A soup combining ingredients from land and sea and eaten as a main course.

capybara
The world's largest rodent—also known as the water pig.

Creole
A type of language based on two or more other languages.

cumfa **(KUM-fah)**
A quasi-religious African dance accompanied by drumming.

jalousie
A system of louvered boards in Guyanese housing design that can be angled differently to allow air to circulate.

jhag **(JAHG)**
A Hindu family thanksgiving, celebrated with religious talks, singing, and feasting.

Kali Mai Puja
An alternative healing practice in Guyana.

kathak **(KAH-tahk)**
A traditional East Indian dance performed by women.

negritude **(nay-gree-TOOD)**
A focus on the contributions of black writers, artists, and thinkers.

pandit
Hindu religious expert.

pork-knockers
Men who spend their lives looking for gold and diamonds in Guyana's interior.

que-que **(kwe-kwe)**
An African dance performed at weddings and other public celebrations.

rajao **(rah-JOWZ)**
A Portuguese banjo.

shirt-jac
Guyanese version of formal dress for men.

sitar
A stringed East Indian musical instrument.

varna **(VAHR-nah)**
One of four groups into which a soul is classified according to religious purity in Hinduism.

FOR FURTHER INFORMATION

BOOKS

Ali, Arif. *Guyana*. Hertford, Hertfordshire: Hansib Publishing Ltd., second edition, 2008.

Browne, Cyril. *Backtracking Through Georgetown, Guyana*. Prosedog.com: RoseDog Books, 2006.

Deryck, Bernard. *Going Home and Other Tales from Guyana*. Oxford: Macmillan Publishers Ltd., 2002.

Kempadoo, Peter Lauchmonen. *Guyana Boy*. Leeds: Peepal Tree Press Ltd., 2003.

Morrison, Marion. *Guyana* (Enchantment of the World Series). Danbury, CT: Scholastic Inc., 2003.

Palmerlee D. and J. Porup. *South America on a Shoestring*. Melbourne: Lonely Planet Publications Pty Ltd., 2007.

Smock, Kirk. *Guyana* (Country Guides) (Bradt Travel Guide). Bucks: Bradt Travel Guides Ltd., first edition, 2008.

FILMS

Jagessar, Rohit. *Guiana 1838*. RBC Radio, 2004.

Wasserman, Suzanne. *Thunder in Guyana*. Independent Lens, 2003.

BIBLIOGRAPHY

BOOKS

Knappert, J. and F. Pelizzoli. *Kings, Gods & Spirits from African Mythology.* New York: Schocken Books, 1986.

Mangru, Basdeo. *Indians in Guyana: A Concise History from Their Arrival to the Present.* Chicago: Adams Press, 1999.

Rosen, Michael. *The Kingfisher Book of Children's Poetry.* New York: Larousse Kingfisher Chambers Inc., 1993.

Zaunders, Bo and Roxie Munro. *Crocodiles, Camels and Dugout Canoes: Eight Adventurous Episodes.* New York: Penguin Group, 1998.

WEBSITES

BBC Production, *Lost Land of the Jaguar: An Expedition to the Jungles of Guyana,* www.bbc.co.uk/sn/tvradio/programmes/jaguar/

CIA Factbook Library on Guyana, www.cia.gov/library/publications/the-world-factbook/geos/gy.html

Climate, www.britannica.com/EBchecked/topic/250021/Guyana

Country profile and time line, http://news.bbc.co.uk/2/hi/americas/country_profiles/1211428.stmCultural Guyana

European discovery and early relations, www.britannica.com/EBchecked/topic/490271/Sir-Walter-Raleigh

Guyana online newspapers, www.ostamyy.com/newspapers.Guyana.htm

Latin American Network Information Center, http://lanic.utexas.edu/la/sa/guyana/

Lonely Planet—Guyana, www.lonelyplanet.com/the-guianas/guyana

Mountainous zone, http://countrystudies.us/guyana/19.htm Newspapers, www.ostamyy.com/newspapers/Guyana.htm

Plants and animals, http://store.saveyourworld.com/category-s/50.htm

Savannah zone, www.stabroeknews.com/2008/business/09/26/prospects-for-sustainable-agro-industrial-investment-in-the-upper-berbice-river-sub-region-2/

Travel adventures, www.traveladventures.org/continents/southamerica/guyana.shtml;

U.S. Department of State on Guyana, www.state.gov/r/pa/ei/bgn/1984.html

INDEX

INDEX